TUBERCULOSIS

TUBERCULOSIS

DIANE YANCEY

Twenty-First Century Medical Library

Twenty-First Century Books
Minneapolis

Twenty-First Century Books
A division of Lerner Publishing Group, Inc.
241 First Avenue North
Minneapolis, MN 55401 U.S.A.

Website address: www.lernerbooks.com

Library of Congress Cataloging-in-Publication Data

Yancey, Diane.
   Tuberculosis / by Diane Yancey. — Rev. ed.
      p.   cm. — (Twenty-first century medical library)
   Includes bibliographical references and index.
   ISBN 978-0-8225-9190-0 (lib. bdg. : alk. paper)
   1. Tuberculosis—Juvenile literature. I. Title.
RC311.Y36 2008
616.9'95—dc22   2007030486

Manufactured in the United States of America
1 2 3 4 5 6 – BP – 13 12 11 10 09 08

CONTENTS

Introduction
TUBERCULOSIS: A PERSISTENT ENEMY
7

Chapter 1
THE WHITE PLAGUE
14

Chapter 2
WHO GETS TB?
30

Chapter 3
SYMPTOMS AND COMPLICATIONS
44

Chapter 4
DIAGNOSIS AND TREATMENT
58

Chapter 5
CHALLENGES TO SOCIETY
78

Chapter 6
ACTION AND AWARENESS
88

Chapter 7
OUTLOOK FOR THE FUTURE
104

————————

GLOSSARY
114

RESOURCES
119

FURTHER READING AND WEBSITES
122

INDEX
124

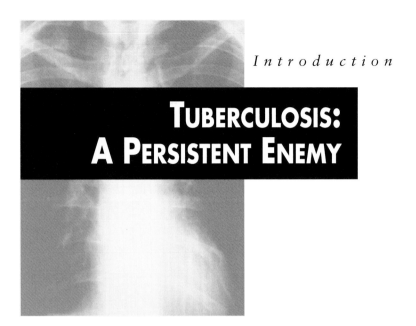

TUBERCULOSIS: A PERSISTENT ENEMY

If you were asked to name the top three infectious killers in the world today, you would probably first think of AIDS (acquired immunodeficiency syndrome), the high-profile scourge that infects nearly 40 million people worldwide and claimed the lives of almost 3 million in 2005 alone. You might guess malaria, which strikes up to 300 million people annually and kills 1 percent of them, making it the third-deadliest disease in the world. It is unlikely, however, that you would think of the world's second-deadliest disease, tuberculosis—an often overlooked disease that passes through the air we breathe and that has infected roughly 2 billion people, about one-third of the world's population.

Tuberculosis (often called TB) is a bacterial infection that usually attacks the lungs but can lodge almost anywhere in the bodies of its victims. TB is remarkable because it can live in the body but remain inactive and cause no symptoms for years—the infection stage—or it can produce symptoms and illness in its active disease stage.

Despite its age-old reputation as a killer, it was not considered a danger to the United States and the Western world during the 1960s, 1970s, and 1980s. Scientific ingenuity and breakthroughs in modern medicine brought its deadly effects under control during those decades. Although it was never eradicated, health officials confidently relegated it to the pages of history along with polio and smallpox.

Their confidence proved unfounded, however. The bacterium *Mycobacterium tuberculosis* mutated easily and quickly became unresponsive to drugs that had once destroyed it. At the same time, changes in society and the world produced conditions that allowed pockets of infection to grow and spread. The result was a resurgence of TB that took health officials by surprise. Once again, the disease became a threat to people of all ages and from every walk of life.

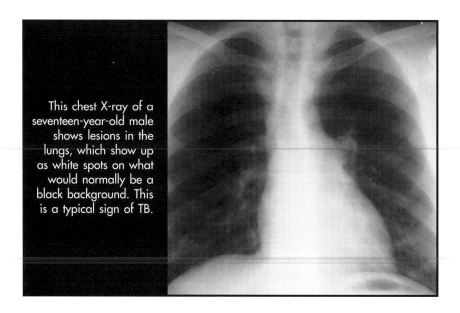

This chest X-ray of a seventeen-year-old male shows lesions in the lungs, which show up as white spots on what would normally be a black background. This is a typical sign of TB.

In this book, you will read about several individuals who have experienced the pain and suffering caused by tuberculosis. Their names and the details of their lives have been changed to preserve their anonymity, but they represent millions who live with and battle the disease every day. Their words reflect the feelings and outlook of people with TB everywhere. Their stories will enable readers to have a better understanding of a disease that manages to survive and disrupt lives just as effectively today as it did hundreds of years ago.

Frédéric, 27 Years Old

Born on the outskirts of Warsaw, Poland, early in the nineteenth century, Frédéric was on his way to becoming a renowned talent in the music world when he developed a stubborn respiratory ailment that would not go away. For years he lived with his symptoms, attributing them to chronic poor health. The fact that he was a bit of a hypochondriac caused his friends to ignore his complaints, which seemed to come and go depending on the weather and his state of mind.

Finally, there was no ignoring the fever and weight loss, and the blood that stained his handkerchief when he coughed. The doctors he visited did not fully understand his illness, which they called phthisis, but they agreed on the gravity of his situation. "One sniffed at what I spat up, the second tapped where I spat it from, the third poked about and listened how I spat it," he wrote to a friend. "One said I had died, the second that I am dying, the third that I shall die."

The prognosis was gloomy, and the young musician guessed that his days of creativity were numbered. Nevertheless, he continued to work and hope, since others he knew lived with the condition.

Perhaps he, too, would be fortunate enough to overcome the odds. If not, the mysterious malady would likely send him to an early grave.

David, 30 Years Old

David, an attorney in the Pacific Northwest, lives in an upscale neighborhood with his wife, Denise, and their two-year-old daughter, Mica. Health minded and athletic, the couple enjoyed skiing, bicycling, and other outdoor sports, until two winters ago, when first David and then the baby came down with what seemed to be bad colds. Unable to shake their symptoms, particularly low-grade fever and a bad cough, they went to their family doctor who diagnosed bronchitis, gave them penicillin, and sent them home to rest and recover.

But two weeks later, they were no better and the doctor wisely decided to take a more careful look at what might be going on in their bodies. His findings astonished everyone.

David and the baby had active cases of tuberculosis. Denise initially tested negative for exposure to the bacteria, but a second test was positive. She showed no symptoms, however. The source of the infection was a mystery, although David vaguely remembered a student at the college he attended being sent home with the disease ten years before.

Randall, 29 Years Old

Randall spends his days wandering city streets looking for ways to support the drug addiction he developed in his mid-twenties. He has a wife and two children, who live in Miami, Florida, and he visits them when he is in the city and when he has a little money to contribute for food.

Randall learned he had HIV (human immuno-deficiency virus) about two years ago. He first started showing signs of active tuberculosis a year later. He went to a free clinic, where he was diagnosed and given a variety of medications, some of which he stopped taking because he disliked the side effects. His TB symptoms disappeared for a time and then reappeared. Clinic personnel know that Randall's lifestyle and his HIV put him at high risk for a strain of tuberculosis that could be deadly to both himself and others. "I appreciate their concern, I really do," Randall says, "but life is tough right now. I'm always on the move, lookin' for work. I know I'm sick, but I got to keep goin'."

Sonia, 23 Years Old

Sonia moved from the Ukraine with her parents when she was a teen, and the family settled in a modest suburban neighborhood near Chicago, Illinois. She became a practical nurse when she finished high school and worked for several years at a Chicago nursing home.

Always prone to respiratory infections, Sonia developed a severe cough one winter and went to her family doctor, who diagnosed a bad cold or the flu. When she failed to recover in a month, however, the physician checked her for tuberculosis. Sonia had active TB, which she may have picked up from family members in the Ukraine. She may also have contracted the infection at work. Some of the residents of the nursing home had the disease, and the facility is not equipped with the latest devices for properly circulating air and quarantining infectious patients.

Jodi, 16 Years Old

Jodi is a California girl, blonde, blue-eyed, and involved in sports and cheerleading at a well-respected high school in the Los Angeles area. She comes from a good home and is not involved in drugs or alcohol, which might make her vulnerable to disease. Yet Jodi was one of several teens to become part of a tuberculosis mini-epidemic that swept her high school. "I was home sick with what we assumed was the flu," she explains. "Then we heard that one of the kids at school had TB. I was tested, and I had it, too. My folks were shocked out of their minds!"

While officials tried to determine where the students contracted the disease, Jodi's parents worried that perhaps she had come in contact with the bacteria while on a vacation. Her father is an airline pilot, and the family is able to travel to countries where tuberculosis is a more common threat. "We've always taken advantage of opportunities to visit other countries and learn about other cultures," her mother explains. "We knew the risk of catching something but discounted it. Now we hear that TB is widespread and incurable in some cases. Should we have put ourselves and our daughter at such a risk?"

All but one of the individuals in the above case studies are fortunate enough to live in the age of antibiotics, when health officials can use drugs to control what at one time could have become an incurable epidemic. Carelessness and neglect of TB for more pressing problems such as cancer, heart disease, and AIDS, however, have again placed everyone at risk for this crippling disease that can involve months of sufferings and can even lead to death.

It has taken time for health officials to understand the factors that are threatening to make the new TB epidemic, in the opinion of some eminent bacteriologists, the greatest public-health disaster since the bubonic plague, a disease that destroyed one-fourth of the population of Europe in the 1300s. As you read on, you will learn what those factors are, as well as who is most at risk to contract the disease, what the symptoms of tuberculosis are, and what people can do to lower their chances of becoming ill. You will also discover how critical the new epidemic really is and to what lengths the global health-care community is going to stem it. First, however, it is important to understand the history of this illness, which is as ancient as the pharaohs and as current as AIDS.

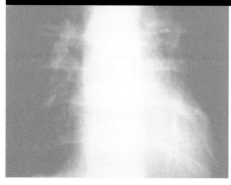

THE WHITE PLAGUE

Frédéric's Story

The young musician was known as the Poet of the Piano in the 1800s for his captivating perform-ances in the drawing rooms of Europe. Today he is remembered as one of the most famous and cre-ative musical composers of all time. But Frédéric Chopin's stellar career was cut tragically short by an insidious illness—tuberculosis—that gradually consumed his body, leaving him pale and lethar-gic, a mere ghost of his former self. "I gasp and cough," he wrote, as the disease progressed. "I have not spat blood since the day before yester-day,—my legs are swollen. . . . I can't go upstairs, I suffocate."

Chopin probably contracted tuberculosis early in his life. One of his sisters died of it when he was young, and he suffered from respiratory problems and bouts of ill health throughout his lifetime. No one recognized the seriousness of his disease until the winter of 1838–1839, when his symptoms grew much worse while he was visiting the island of Majorca. Doctors confirmed that he had phthisis—the name for tuberculosis at that time—but no cure existed. The once-energetic young Chopin grew increasingly frail and weak, until he died of his illness in 1849 at the age of thirty-nine.

Chopin's friend, the composer Franz Liszt, wrote of the painful, drawn-out death that was typical of the disease. "His youthful loveliness, so long dimmed by bitter sufferings, was restored by death, and among the flowers he loved, he slept his long, last, dreamless sleep." Had he lived one hundred years later, Chopin might have been saved by physicians who would have known that his killer was a strain of bacteria and who could have used a newly discovered "miracle drug" to stop the disease in its tracks and preserve the life of the young composer.

DISEASE OF THE ANCIENTS

Frédéric Chopin was by no means the first human being to fall victim to tuberculosis. Historical evidence shows that the disease has infected humans for as many as ten thousand years. Signs of it have been found in skeletons from the Neolithic Age, a period ranging from 8000 to about 2000 B.C. Mummified remains uncovered in Egypt indicate that tuberculosis sanitoriums, or hospitals, may have existed in that country as far back as 3000 B.C. Babylonian tablets written more than two thousand years ago describe symptoms of the disease. And while historians know that sweeping epidemics of tuberculosis in the Western world had their start with European explorers, evidence shows

Frédéric Chopin died young from tuberculosis in 1849. Had he lived about one hundred years later, there is a good chance that he would have been cured of the disease.

that the disease affected Native Americans even before that time. TB germs have been found in a Peruvian mummy dating from before the time of Columbus.

Ancient Romans, Hindus, and Greeks all refer to tuberculosis in their writings, the latter calling it *phthisis*, "to shrivel up and waste away." The disease was given a variety of other names as it accompanied mankind into more modern times—consumption, the King's Evil, the wasting disease, scrofula, and the White Plague, the latter referring to the pallor of TB victims. The designation "tuberculosis" was first used about 1839 and came from the Latin word *tubercula*, meaning "small lump." The term refers to the small boils seen in tissues of infected individuals.

ROMANTIC CONSUMPTION

Tuberculosis has manifested itself in many forms over time, destroying people's lungs, causing their bones to deteriorate, their lymph nodes to swell and drain, and their skin to thicken and break out into sores. It took time for doctors to realize that what they thought was a variety of diseases was in fact a single one. In its many manifestations, tuberculosis remained a leading cause of death through the centuries, particularly with the growth of cities where populations were more dense and opportunities for infection greater. In the 1600s, one out of every four deaths in Europe was due to TB.

In the eighteenth and nineteenth centuries, tuberculosis assumed epidemic proportions in Europe. "There is no more dangerous disease than pulmonary phthisis, and no other is so common. . . . It destroys a very great part of the human race," wrote Antoine Portal of France at the beginning of the nineteenth century. Nineteenth-century medical records in England show that about half of the country's population had scrofula, tuberculosis of the lymph nodes.

Despite its destructiveness, tuberculosis had a certain glamorous reputation because many well-known, artistic individuals suffered from it. In addition to Chopin, composer Wolfgang Amadeus Mozart, poets John Keats and Edgar Allan Poe, and authors Charlotte and Emily Brontë, Henry David Thoreau, and Ralph Waldo Emerson were victims of the disease. So great were the numbers that many people believed that a link existed between tuberculosis and creativity; that perhaps it was an inherited trait that went hand-in-hand with genius; or that it somehow helped writers, musicians, and artists to reach greater heights in their work.

There was no truth to the speculations. Artistic individuals contracted TB at the same rate as the general population, and many artists were healthy and robust. Nevertheless, tuberculosis grew so prestigious that a pale, wasted appearance became fashionable among many upper-class young women, who believed it gave them a look of spirituality, refinement, and purity. Some people, like British poet Lord Byron, who also had tuberculosis, even considered it romantic to bravely suffer a lingering death from the disease. "I should like to die of consumption," he wrote in 1828. "The ladies would all say, 'Look at that poor Byron, how interesting he looks in dying!'"

While romantic to some, death from tuberculosis was a grim, painful experience, and the disease was deeply feared by many, since no one knew how to prevent or cure it. Entire families had difficulty making good marriages, were barred from certain occupations, and had life insurance claims rejected on the basis of a history of infection. In some regions, residents correctly recognized tuberculosis to be contagious and passed laws regulating its treatment. When Chopin wintered on the island of Majorca in 1838–1839, his friend George Sand wrote:

> *After a month there, poor Chopin's disease got worse, and we called in one, two, then three physicians . . . who spread through the Island the news that their patient was suffering from the lungs. The tale stirred up great terror. Phthisis is scarce in these climates and is regarded as contagious. . . . The owner of our small house threw us out immediately and started a suit to compel us to replaster his house on the pretext that we had contaminated it.*

DISEASE OF THE MASSES

As time passed and more people moved to cities, where they often lived in overcrowded tenements, suffered malnutrition and poverty, and fell prey to all kinds of infectious complaints, tuberculosis lost its high-class reputation and became known as a disease of the masses. Celebrated French researchers Jean and René Dubos wrote in their book *The White Plague*, "A great outburst of disease followed the Industrial Revolution. The epidemic became the White Plague, giving pallor to the dreariness of the mushrooming cities, and injecting its fever into the romantic mood of the age." Millions of workers and their families carried out their daily routines while breathing, blowing, coughing, and spitting deadly TB germs wherever they went. By 1907 over 150,000 people died annually of the disease in the United States alone.

Terrified of the threat that tuberculosis posed, the public began to take action. Some even panicked. Employers fired employees who were ill. Barbers refused to shave men who had TB. Public-health crusaders began a movement to educate the country on how to control and prevent the disease. The National Association for the Study and Prevention of Tuberculosis was formed in the United States in 1904, with similar organizations being founded in Europe. People were instructed to boil any milk they drank (milk was a major source of infection at the time), to quit their jobs or stay home from school if they became infected, and to rest and get plenty of fresh air. René Dubos describes other standards of the movement. "Spitting in public places was taught to be a manifestation of bad taste, unguarded sneezing an antisocial act. Access to fresh air and sunshine became a natural right, good health almost a duty." No-spitting ordinances were passed in many cities, and no-spitting signs were displayed in prominent places. Cleanup crews were hired to disinfect sidewalks and public places where infected individuals were likely to pass.

Those who were dedicated to fighting TB soon grew impatient with the carelessness of the public, particularly the lower class. One worker observed, "People of this class are by nature weak, shiftless, and lacking in initiative and perseverance. They have neither inherited nor acquired moral strength . . . and are often vicious besides." Since racial minorities, particularly blacks and Native Americans, came down with the disease in high numbers, tuberculosis became a justification for discrimination. (The TB mortality rate for Native Americans was seven times higher than for the general population in 1912, and that of African Americans, two to three times higher than for Caucasians.) Someone with tuberculosis was now seen as sinful, inferior, and a menace to society.

In this atmosphere, it seemed logical for the government to take stern steps to control the further spread of tuberculosis. In 1905 the U.S. Supreme Court ruled that compulsory vaccination was legal, even though no effective vaccine against TB was then available. The U.S. Commission of Immigration closed the nation's doors to immigrants who exhibited symptoms of the disease. Mandatory cattle inspections were instituted to eliminate milk as a source of infection. Hospitals were told to isolate tubercular patients, and health departments were forced to give the names and addresses of infected clients so they could be tracked down. Some patients were sent to sanitoriums to recover or die. Those who refused were sometimes forcibly incarcerated in primitive and overcrowded state-financed institutions such as the Riverside Sanatorium on North Brother Island in New York Harbor or the Otisville Sanatorium in New York City. At the latter, patients were compelled to undergo the "work cure," a demanding form of therapy based on the presumption that public funds would be saved if poor TB victims were put to work to help support themselves.

"CURES" THROUGH THE AGES

Isolation was only one of many methods tried over the years to control or cure tuberculosis. In the fourth century B.C., the Greek physician Hippocrates believed that cleanliness and a healthy diet were proper treatments. Galen, another Greek physician of a slightly later era, recommended smearing patients' feet with butter after first wiping them with myrrh oil steeped with a potion of the herb lupine. Pliny the Elder, the foremost scientific thinker in Rome in the first century A.D., believed that "the flesh of a she-ass taken with broth" or "the ashes of swine-dung mixed into raisin wine," would bring about healing. Other ancient Romans relied on wolf's liver, elephant blood, or bathing in the urine of someone who had eaten cabbage. In early England and France, the touch of the king or queen was said to cure the disease.

In the 1800s, various quacks and charlatans became rich treating well-to-do patients with remedies such as a solution of brown sugar and water, warm air and sulfuric acid, or syrup made from millipedes. Chopin's sister Emilia suffered through harsher treatments, which shocked and terrified her brother. "They bled her once, twice; leeches without end, vesicators [blistering agents], sinapisms [mustard plasters], wolf's-bane [medicinal herbs]; horrors, horrors!" Doctors of the time also experimented with starvation, overfeeding, bed rest, extensive exercise, and opium. The latter was widely used in the nineteenth century to quiet coughs and quell diarrhea brought on by intestinal tuberculosis. Each cure had its supporters, but no treatment went to the root of the problem—the tiny bacteria that lay deep within the lungs and tissues of tuberculosis sufferers.

Despite a lack of scientific knowledge, some progress was made toward understanding the disease as years passed. In 1546 an Italian named Girolamo Fracastoro noticed that tuberculosis usually attacked the lungs and suggested that it might be contagious, with the causative agent carried on clothing or in the air. Most of the European medical community scoffed at the possibility, but the evidence seemed strong to one astute British physician, Benjamin Marten. In 1722 he wrote:

It may, therefore, be very likely that by habitual lying in the same Bed with a consumptive Patient, constantly eating and drinking with him or by very

frequently conversing so nearly as to draw in part
of the Breath he emits from the Lungs, a Con-
sumption may be caught by a sound person.

KOCH'S DISCOVERY

Finally, in the mid-1800s, the contagionist theory began to gain wide support in Europe. A French surgeon, Jean-Antoine Villemin, proved that TB was contagious by infecting guinea pigs and rabbits from sputum and blood taken from sick humans and cattle. His findings were supported by other scientists, notably the British epidemiologist William Budd, who studied consumption in Africans. Budd discovered that those who had contact with Europeans had a high death rate while those who lived farther inland and had little contact with Europeans remained virtually TB free.

Definite proof of the contagionist theory was found in 1882, when Robert Koch of Germany discovered the rod-shaped bacterium that caused tuberculosis. His isolation of a different bacteria type called anthrax had established the "germ theory" of disease in the 1870s, proving that illnesses were not caused by mysterious substances but by microorganisms. In a carefully thought-out series of experiments, the German scientist identified the tuberculosis bacterium (later named *Mycobacterium tuberculosis*), cultured it in his laboratory, and then produced the disease by inoculating animals with the culture. Koch was awarded the Nobel Prize in medicine in 1905 for his breakthrough work in tuberculosis.

The cause of the "White Plague" was now identified, but a cure had not yet been found. Koch himself put forth his own remedy in 1890—a simple glycerin extract of dead bacilli (bacteria), which he called tuberculin. It proved ineffective, and in some cases, it made patients sicker than those who remained untreated. Koch's extract, however, later became the basis for skin testing to determine whether or not patients had been exposed to *M. tuberculosis*.

Robert Koch discovered many bacteria responsible for disease, including anthrax and cholera. His most famous success, in 1882, was the isolation of the bacteria that caused tuberculosis. At the time, tuberculosis was the cause of one in seven deaths in Europe.

The search for a cure continued. Again, a variety of remedies came on the market, including vaccines that promised to protect from infection and treatments that guaranteed miraculous recoveries. Injecting sufferers with gold salts was one option. Taking creosote, a derivative of coal tar commonly used as a preservative and disinfectant, was another. One patient wrote to his physician, "Dr. I have to stop taking creosote it upset my stomach so and I have tried it several times. . . . Now Dr. if I am not imposing on you, can you send me a prescription to stop hemorrhages [bleeding]?" Thoracoplasty, the surgical removal of part of a patient's ribs, was popular for a time, as was the notion of treatment in a TB sanitorium, which swept the medical community beginning in the 1880s.

THE AGE OF SANITORIUMS

The belief that rest and a healthful climate, complete with plenty of fresh air and sunshine, could cure tuberculosis was a time-honored one, probably based on the observation that country dwellers got sick from the disease less often than did those who lived in the city. Romans in A.D. 200 were some of the first to recognize this characteristic of the disease, and tuberculosis sufferers were often sent on long ocean voyages in hopes that sea breezes and salt air would improve their condition. René Dubos points to the fact that "Many English consumptives of the nineteenth century voyaged in Southern waters, encouraged by the memory of ancient medical traditions."

Hermann Brehmer, a German doctor who had recovered from the disease while on a plant-collecting expedition to the Himalaya mountains, was motivated by the belief that fresh air and rest could cure tuberculosis. In 1859 he established the first modern TB sanitorium—part hospital, part open-air hotel—in eastern Europe. Edward Livingston Trudeau, a consumptive American physician who had planned to spend his final days in the

Adirondack Mountains, found that his symptoms disappeared in the fresh air. He opened the first American tuberculosis sanitorium in Saranac Lake, New York, in 1885. The facility became the model for over six hundred sanitoriums that sprang up across the U.S. landscape and became the keystone of TB treatment for thousands of sufferers.

The basis of sanitorium life was organization and optimism. Daily activity—from brushing teeth to talking to reading—was regulated and controlled. Positive thinking was encouraged. Death was never mentioned. Even in the middle of winter, patients spent time swathed in blankets on chaise lounges on patios and in front of open windows,

Young tuberculosis patients got plenty of fresh air and sunshine, popular treatments at that time, at a sanitorium in Cleveland, Ohio, in 1918.

breathing in fresh air, soaking up all the sunshine they could get. Rest and a healthy diet helped their bodies fight the disease, ultraviolet rays from the sun helped kill the germs they exhaled, and their stays isolated them from uninfected individuals on the outside. Despite these well-intentioned efforts, they received no real benefits, and later studies showed that people treated in sanitoriums died at the same rate as those who remained at home. Nevertheless, sanitoriums remained a mainstay of treatment well into the mid-twentieth century.

ANTIBIOTIC THERAPY

A turning point in the history of tuberculosis came in 1943, when a poultry farmer in New Jersey noted that his chickens were falling ill with a mysterious malady. Investigation of the barnyard soil revealed a fungus that was later determined to have properties other than the capacity for making chickens sick. Laboratory investigation demonstrated that the fungus, *Streptomyces griseus*, produced a chemical agent that slowed the growth of some disease-causing bacteria. The agent, described in 1944 by the American soil biologist Selman Waksman, is now known as streptomycin. It proved to be the first compound that effectively killed tuberculosis bacteria. Waksman won the Nobel Prize for his discovery in 1952.

Streptomycin was not a perfect antibiotic. It had side effects, and tuberculosis bacteria developed resistance to it in a relatively short time, making it ineffective in long-term treatment. Eventually, however, other antibiotics were developed—isoniazid in the 1950s, ethambutol in the 1960s, and rifampicin in the 1970s. These worked in combination with streptomycin or with one another.

As antibiotic therapy replaced all other cures, deaths from TB plummeted in the United States from 188 per 100,000 people in 1904 to 1 per 100,000 by 1980. TB sanitoriums closed for lack of patients. Funding for

Selman Waksman was instrumental in discovering at least nine antibiotics in the 1940s. One of these, streptomycin, was the first antibiotic used to treat tuberculosis.

research and for public-health programs designed to prevent and treat TB was drastically cut. The disease remained a problem among the poor, but the medical community complacently believed that they had conquered the dreaded killer and needed only to put forth a little effort to permanently eradicate it.

REBIRTH OF A KILLER

Contrary to all expectations, tuberculosis was a killer that evaded its own death. To the amazement of the health community, beginning in 1985, people with tuberculosis began showing up in increasing numbers at hospitals and clinics in the United States and around the world. In 1990 the United States had nearly a 10 percent increase in TB cases over the previous year, the largest annual increase since such records were first kept in 1953.

Large cities such as Los Angeles, Miami, and New York City were sites of the worst outbreaks, and many cases were resistant to standard antibiotic treatment. Soon eight million new active cases of TB were being recorded throughout the world every year, and three million people were dying annually. By 1999 it was estimated that almost two billion of the world's six billion people were infected with the bacteria worldwide. Ten to fifteen million of those cases (about one-quarter of 1 percent of the world's population) occurred in the United States, with about twenty thousand new cases showing up annually.

What caused such a rebound, when TB seemed to be a waning threat? Negligence was one of the most crucial factors. Never completely eliminated, TB had been all but ignored by health-care officials whose time and money were taken up fighting more conspicuous diseases such as AIDS and cancer. "We had everything we needed. All the knowledge, the skills, the medical expertise necessary to eliminate this disease. Instead, this country chose to very nearly eliminate the health-care programs people with this disease need most," says Dr. Barry R. Bloom, a TB specialist in New York.

Improper treatment was another factor. It allowed the toughest bacteria to survive and multiply until new strains were all but unaffected by available medications. Complications such as AIDS, immigration, drug abuse, and poverty added to the problem of care and control, with the result that the medical community faced an epidemic that was as complex as it was deadly.

NEW EFFORTS

Taken by surprise, health organizations in the United States and throughout the world rallied in the 1990s to try to fight the upsurge of TB infection. Their efforts will be detailed in later chapters of this book. To understand those efforts, however, a profile of who is at greatest risk for tuberculosis today is needed. The next chapter will give more information about those who are in danger of infection, those who are likely to develop active TB, and those who have a high chance of dying from the disease. "TB's not just a disease of the poor and homeless," suburbanites David and Denise point out. "People don't have a sense yet of just how serious the problem really is. 'Think TB' is a very good motto for everyone to follow today."

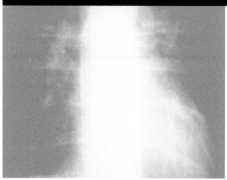

WHO GETS TB?

David's Story

David, an attorney in the Pacific Northwest, grew up in an ordinary middle-class family in a small town in central California. In his youth, he attended a small private academy rather than the local public school, where migrant and minority children made up a large part of the student body. "I wasn't a pampered kid, but my folks had notions about the right side and the wrong side of the tracks," David remembers. "Mom was also afraid I'd catch something from the 'outsiders' as she called them, so she put us in private school."

After graduation from high school, David attended a nearby university. During his four years there, a student who lived in a dorm across campus was diagnosed with tuberculosis and sent home to recover. As far as David knows, he never came in contact with that student. "But who knows?" he says with a shrug. "Maybe he was the guy that sat behind me in English 101 all semester, breathing down the back of my neck. Maybe he hung out at the burger joint where I spent a lot of time. They say TB is pretty hard to catch, but there are always stories that prove the exception."

David might have contracted TB anytime in the past, since the bacteria can lay dormant in the human body for many years before developing into active disease. His doctor has no idea why the young attorney got sick when he did, however. He had seldom been ill in his lifetime. After daughter Mica was born, his wife Denise, a former nurse, had been extra careful of the family's health. She insisted that they avoid people with colds, take vitamins, and get plenty of rest. When David wanted to volunteer with other members of their church to serve Thanksgiving dinner at a homeless shelter, Denise vetoed his plans, pointing out that shelters can be havens for disease.

Despite such caution, David came down with TB and passed it to Mica. "It's ironic," he says. "We were so careful, and Mica and I got sick anyway. I guess I'm grateful that our doctor diagnosed it fairly quickly. But I felt so guilty when Mica cried when she had to take her medicine. I caused her suffering, there's no getting around it."

WHO CAN GET TUBERCULOSIS?

As David's story illustrates, anyone can get tuberculosis. Although few healthy middle-class people contract the disease, a growing number of suburban families and other ordinary able-bodied individuals have been unexpectedly infected in recent times. For instance, in 1992 two employees of a business in the World Trade Center in New York City were diagnosed with tuberculosis, and staff members had to undergo TB skin tests before they were allowed back on the job. In 1998 a communications specialist in Arizona developed a resistant strain of the bacteria and needed radical surgery before she could recover. And in 2005, a junior doctor at Boston Medical Center in Massachusetts developed TB. More than five hundred health-care workers and patients at the center had to be tested for the disease.

In theory, tuberculosis is easy to catch. The bacteria commonly infect the lungs. When the disease is active, germs are carried out of the body on droplets of moisture whenever the victim coughs, sneezes, talks, sings, or spits. It takes only one or two of these bacteria to cause a new infection. One observer points out "Perhaps the question we all should be asking is not "why do so many people get TB,' but 'why aren't we all infected if the disease is so easy to pass?'"

In reality, catching TB is not as easy as it sounds—a person with active, untreated TB will infect only ten to fifteen people each year. In the presence of a contagious individual, the chances of becoming infected after only casual contact are very slight, far less than the risk of catching a cold. TB cannot be caught from clothes, tabletops, toys, or other items touched by a person with the disease. Risks are extremely low outdoors where ultraviolet light from the sun kills bacteria in about an hour and where germs can disperse in the open air.

Tuberculosis is most likely to be contracted in crowded, unventilated conditions. Overcrowded tenement buildings, prisons, and long-term care facilities can be perfect settings for transmission and infection. Indoor locales such as subways, restaurants, and doctors' offices pose only moderate risks, because most people need prolonged exposure before they are infected. Experts point out that it takes an average of two months of round-the-clock contact or six months of eight-hour-a-day contact with someone with untreated active tuberculosis for a person to become infected. Even then the body's natural resistance prevents the vast majority of those infected from developing an active case of tuberculosis.

WHO IS MOST AT RISK?

Persons who are in contact with infectious individuals for significant lengths of time have a 30 to 50 percent chance of becoming infected with tuberculosis. One-tenth of those who are infected will develop the disease during their lifetime. Those who run the greatest risk of getting tuberculosis include the following:

Family, Friends, and Colleagues

Tuberculosis is commonly passed among family members and between those who work together, particularly if conditions are crowded and poorly ventilated. Prolonged contact that comes with sharing airspace—living with one's family or working side by side with someone every day—is necessary to spread infection from person to person.

The Elderly

Older people are at risk for developing tuberculosis because many were exposed to TB decades ago when the disease was more prevalent. They have carried the inactive bacteria in their lungs for years, and as age weakens their immune systems, their bodies are no longer as able to fight off the disease. "I tested positive for infection after working in a TB ward as a nurse during World War Two [1939–1945]," says one eighty-year-old woman who recently came down with active tuberculosis. "I didn't get sick then, and after all those years I figured there was no risk. Guess my unlucky number just came up."

Factors such as malnutrition or chronic health problems among the elderly may lower resistance and permit an onset of TB. Untreated health problems can also contribute to activation of the disease. Some elderly people cannot afford medical care or do not have a way to get to the doctor. Their health can deteriorate to the point where they risk illness.

Older people in nursing homes and other long-term care facilities are at even greater risk of catching or developing tuberculosis than their counterparts who live at home. Nursing-home patients may be prone to illness and usually remain indoors, where prolonged exposure to disease can take place. Health-care staff may be lax about testing patients for TB infection. They may fail to recognize symptoms, ascribing weight loss, cough, and weakness to other diseases such as pneumonia or to aging itself.

Even doctors can miss diagnosing the disease, since symptoms are usually subtle. Few elderly patients complain of night sweats or cough up blood, symptoms that are typical of TB in younger patients. "I tried to tell them I was feeling *bad*," says an eighty-year-old from behind the mask he now wears, despite the fact that antibiotics have controlled his infection. "It wasn't till my daughter came for a visit and took me to her doctor that I found out I had TB. Then they told me I'd infected a couple of my neighbors down the hall. You can bet that slowed down my chances for a good game of checkers."

The Seriously Ill

Any person with a health condition that weakens the immune system and undermines resistance is at risk for catching and developing tuberculosis. Such conditions include silicosis and lung cancer, both of which damage lung tissue. Individuals with leukemia and Hodgkin's disease (cancer of the lymphatic system) are at risk, as are those with diabetes and severe kidney disease. "Denise has a diabetic aunt who loves to baby-sit Mica," David says. "We were afraid she'd get sick and maybe have all sorts of complications. It was a real relief when her skin test was negative!"

Individuals with extremely low body weight are also at risk for tuberculosis, since they may be malnourished. So are those who have had organ transplants and take immune suppressing drugs to prevent their bodies from rejecting the new organs. Without a strong immune system, they are susceptible to many infections, including TB.

People with HIV and AIDS

Persons with HIV and AIDS are at extremely high risk for contracting TB. A person with HIV gradually loses immune function in his body as the virus destroys cells that fight infection. When the immune system is almost

TB HIV

Double Trouble

People with HIV Infection face a greater risk of also developing TB.
Don't take chances. Get tested.

Call your physician or county health department for a tuberculosis test today
— especially if you know you're HIV-infected.

This Mississippi State Department of Health poster from 1992 stresses the risk of contracting TB for those who have HIV. Tuberculosis infections rose dramatically in the United States in the early 1990s.

totally suppressed, that person has AIDS and can easily develop a variety of potentially deadly opportunistic infections, including pneumonia, cancer, fungus infections, and tuberculosis.

HIV and AIDS have proved to be significant contributing factors in the upswing in tuberculosis infection throughout the world. Complicating the problem is the fact that some people with HIV and AIDS are drug addicts or homeless individuals who are already vulnerable to infection and can be careless about getting medical help. "I don't always keep my doctors appointments," says Randall, who has HIV and TB and sleeps on the street. "When I'm feeling sick, the last thing I need is to walk six blocks to a clinic, sit on a folding chair in their waiting room for a couple of hours, and then listen to the nurse badger me about not taking my medicine."

Only one out of ten normally healthy individuals who is infected with tuberculosis will develop the disease over the course of a lifetime. That risk rises dramatically for those with both TB infection and HIV, however. In such cases, an average of one out of ten persons will develop active TB *each year*. AIDS patients who become infected with TB have a 50 percent chance of developing active TB within the first year of infection. Particularly dangerous is infection with drug-resistant strains of the organism, which can kill an AIDS patient in as little as two months.

The AIDS/TB epidemic will be discussed in greater detail in chapter 3.

The Poor

Poor people suffer more from health problems including tuberculosis than do individuals with adequate incomes. Although it is difficult to obtain accurate figures, it is estimated that between 6 and 7 percent of all people with TB in the United States are homeless and that active cases of the disease are nearly twenty times more prevalent among the homeless than in the nation as a whole.

The high numbers stem from a variety of factors. Many of the poor cannot afford adequate housing and so live and sleep in unsanitary, overcrowded conditions where TB is easily passed from person to person. They may live in abandoned buildings or on the streets. Some take advantage of shelters, where TB is easily passed between people sleeping in close proximity to one another. "I like shelters, but sometimes all the coughing and moaning at night disturbs my rest," Randall says. "I do my share of coughing, too, and I have to think that the guys around me in the room are just as ticked off at me as I am with them."

Many of the poor are malnourished. Many are drug users and/or alcoholics who are careless with their health. The majority have little or no access to healthcare, never see a doctor, and may even avoid authorities if they have had run-ins with the law. One category of the poor—migrant workers and their families—seldom stay in one place long enough to utilize medical treatment except in extreme emergencies (their wages may be docked if they take time from work to seek treatment). "If they can't get attention for a broken leg, they sure won't get it for a cough," says one authority on migrant workers.

Minorities

Certain minorities including African Americans, Hispanics, and Native Americans are at high risk for catching TB, and the progression of the disease from onset to severe illness is often more rapid for these groups than for Caucasians. This is because larger numbers of minorities are poor and share conditions such as homelessness, poor nutrition, and little or no access to health care that are common to other economically impoverished groups at risk for TB.

Experts believe that another factor—genetic history—could play a role in minorities' greater susceptibility as well. For thousands of years, tuberculosis existed in epidemic proportions in Europe, a region primarily populated by Caucasians. Those individuals who were more resistant to the disease survived and reproduced, passing on their resistant genes to generations that followed. Ancestors of blacks, Hispanics, and Asians, however, did not encounter TB to such an extent until much later in history, and thus have had less time to develop and pass on tuberculosis-resistant genes to subsequent generations.

Whether because of social or genetic factors, statistics show that more than 50 percent of TB cases in the United States in 2004 were among African American and Hispanic groups, while another 23 percent were found among Asians.

Children

The number of children with tuberculosis rose alarmingly in the United States in the last part of the twentieth century. Between 1988 and 1990, at the height of the epidemic, the Centers for Disease Control and Prevention (CDC) documented a 41 percent increase in cases of tuberculosis among children under the age of fifteen. Efforts by health officials have since resulted in a dramatic decrease in cases nationwide, but among some demographic groups (such as the poor, migrants, and some minorities), the problem of finding and treating infected youngsters remains acute.

Almost all children who contract TB do so from an adult with whom they live or are around regularly. Children under the age of five are among those at highest risk for developing active TB because their immune systems are not fully developed and they have not yet had time to build resistance. Statistics show that almost half of children under the age of one who are infected with TB develop active disease if they do not get preventive therapy. Children with active disease are not as infectious as adults, however, since they rarely develop cavities (pockets of diseased tissue with high concentrations of bacteria) in their lungs. "We were concerned that Mica may have infected the kids in the church nursery," David says, "but

This Kenyan woman and her baby *(left)* are both HIV positive and suffering from TB. Her daughter *(right)* is the only one in the family still healthy. Children who have TB most often catch the disease from their parents or other adults they see frequently.

the doctor explained that she had few bacteria in her sputum, and was only in the nursery for an hour on Sunday, so everyone was at fairly low risk. I think some of the mothers had their kids tested, though."

Health-Care Workers

Healthy-care workers, including those in hospitals, clinics, rest homes, and other long-term care facilities, are at high risk of becoming infected with tuberculosis, particularly with drug-resistant strains that are difficult to cure. At lease sixteen health-care workers in the United States. became infected with multidrug-resistant TB (MDR-TB) at the peak of the epidemic in the early 1990s, and five died as a result of the disease.

The magnitude of risk for health-care workers depends on the prevalence of TB in their community, the type of facility in which they work, and how effectively disease is controlled in that facility. Nursing homes and even hospitals may lack isolation rooms and may be improperly ventilated. Tubercular patients may not be required to wear protective masks when they leave their rooms. Health workers who carry out certain medical procedures that have to do with the lungs, such as endotracheal intubation and bronchoscopy, may be at higher risk than staff members who work in areas such as reception or food service.

Prison Staff

Prison staff, whose clientele are often poor and careless with their health, face dangers similar to those faced by health-care workers when they come in repeated and prolonged contact with tubercular inmates. Correctional facilities are often overcrowded and may have inferior medical services and facilities. Workers are sometimes improperly trained and do not follow appropriate procedures to contain infection. Many are slow about identifying infected inmates, slow to isolate them, and slow to provide treatment, with the result that contagious individuals spread their germs throughout the wards and to the staff. Those who are released with incompletely treated infections can also spread disease to family and friends.

Immigrants

Tuberculosis is very prevalent in some undeveloped countries, and increased tourism, business travel, and immigration heighten the risk of contracting disease from those locales. In many industrialized countries such as the United States, almost one-half of tuberculosis cases are among the foreign-born. Babies adopted from Siberia are often infected with multidrug resistant TB. Students from Southeast Asia sometimes infect their peers at school. Nannies from South America may infect their employers' family members. Many immigrants who are not infectious when they enter a country may become infectious as time passes.

Tubercular immigrants may not get proper treatment for their disease even after they enter countries that provide good health care. Many are poor, and many are not used to going to doctors. Many stay away from doctors and clinics because they cannot speak English and communication barriers seem insurmountable. For those who do seek treatment, records from home countries are often unavailable so that health workers cannot determine how long the patient has been infected, if prior treatment existed and was effective, or if other contacts abroad were infected and are spreading the disease. Immigrants who are diagnosed and given medication may not be able to understand instructions, may fail to take medicine correctly, and may not return for subsequent treatments. Health officials have difficulty following up on infected individuals who come in once and then disappear leaving no permanent address.

THE GLOBAL RISK

Tuberculosis is the same disease no matter where it appears, and high-risk groups around the world are similar to those found in the United States. The difference is essentially in the numbers of those infected. Ninety-five percent of the world's cases of active TB occur in developing countries. In some countries in Africa, the incidence of tuberculosis has doubled since the 1980s. The higher numbers could be attributed, in part, to improved reporting of cases. However, great poverty and ignorance, inadequate health facilities, poor access to health facilities, and lack of funds set aside to control and prevent infection have certainly contributed to an increase in cases. War, famine, ethnic persecution, and the like also encourage higher infection rates. People who are forced from their homes often gather in shelters or refugee camps where the disease can spread from person to person faster than in ordinary circumstances.

Even under stable conditions, social and health practices in developing countries aggravate the TB problem. The worldwide AIDS epidemic impairs people's health and makes them particularly susceptible to TB infection. Over-the-counter antibiotics, available without doctor's prescription in some countries, allow TB patients to take just enough medicine to feel better, but not to kill all the germs they carry. Ineffective treatment leads to drug-resistant strains, and some countries are developing large numbers of virtually incurable cases. In an age of air travel, such resistant strains are easily carried from place to place. For instance, in May 2007, American businessman Andrew Speaker flew from the United States to Europe and back after having been diagnosed with drug resistant TB. The Centers for Disease Control and Prevention (CDC) had warned Speaker to avoid travel, but he discounted the warning. Although no one who came into contact with him has yet been diagnosed with TB, the case is still being monitored closely.

Eastern Europe is one region that reports a significant number of resistant cases of TB. Other potential trouble spots include China, Bangladesh, India, Indonesia, Pakistan, and the Philippines. Russia and other former Soviet states report high failure rates for treatment, a condition that can indicate resistant strains. "Even in rich countries, efforts to fight TB are severely hampered by the lack of effective tools," said Dr. Peter Small, the senior program officer for tuberculosis at the Bill and Melinda Gates Foundation, a charitable foundation that has donated more than $700 million to fighting tuberculosis. "Better vaccines, diagnostics, and drugs could dramatically improve the fight against TB, especially in poor countries where large numbers of people are affected by the disease."

Physicians such as Small fully comprehend the threat tuberculosis poses to the world, as well as the mechanisms by which *M. tuberculosis* survives and spreads in vulnerable populations. Discussion of tuberculosis can be confusing,

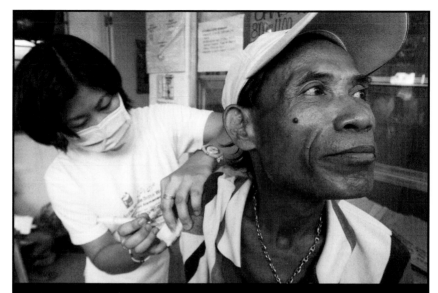

A man receives a TB shot in one of the poorest neighborhoods in Manila, Philippines. In the early 2000s, this neighborhood experienced at least one new case of TB every day due to the appearance of new drug-resistant strains.

however, if one does not clearly understand the meaning of terms such as *resistance*, *infection*, *latency*, *disease*, and *active case* and if one is not familiar with the process by which TB bacilli infect the human body once they enter it. The disease, its symptoms, and the complications that can occur when someone gets sick will be discussed in detail in the next chapter.

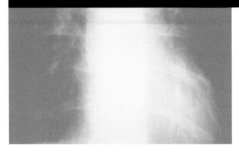

Chapter 3

SYMPTOMS AND COMPLICATIONS

Randall's Story

Randall is not yet thirty years old, but with his gaunt body, bent shoulders, and weathered face, he looks closer to fifty. His clothes are grimy. He has lived on the streets of Miami, Chicago, Los Angeles, and a dozen other cities. His most prized possession is a secondhand down sleeping bag, which he carries rolled on his back. It is his bed, his shelter, and his primary place of residence, although when he is in Miami, he spends the night with his wife and children, who live in a small apartment in the suburbs.

Randall's daily routine usually includes doing odd jobs for people at various homeless shelters and panhandling a few dollars on the street. He uses the money for drugs or alcohol. On days that he's sober, he talks to friends about his children and his dreams for their future. One of those dreams includes buying a farm somewhere in New England so his kids can have a dog.

Randall knows, however, that his dreams are unlikely to come true. He's already beginning to experience fatigue and other symptoms of AIDS. He also has symptoms of active tuberculosis—a wracking cough, weight loss, and night sweats. "I got AIDS from a dirty needle," he says unemotionally. "I think I got TB from one of the men's shelters where I stay now and then. A doctor told me shelters can be pretty dangerous—that outdoors is healthier—but he never tried sleeping on the sidewalk, so he doesn't know."

Randall's tuberculosis was first diagnosed at a health clinic in Chicago, where he was given three standard antibiotics and told to return for followup. "I hate those pills," Randall complains. "I had trouble swallowing them, and they made me feel bad. I pretty much stopped taking two of the three after a week, although I didn't tell the doc that."

Randall's symptoms improved temporarily and then returned a few months later. By then he was living in the Los Angeles area, spending his days in a park and nights in an abandoned building. When asked by a nurse at an emergency clinic about previous treatment, Randall claimed he couldn't remember and was given the same three antibiotics. He took them only until his symptoms subsided, so the most resistant of his bacteria remained alive in his system. Soon his symptoms returned, more troublesome than ever.

Randall was visibly ill and highly infectious with TB as he made his way from Los Angeles to Miami to visit his children. His coughing spells disturbed fellow bus passengers and drew recommendations from the driver that he get some cough drops. When Randall went to a health clinic at his wife's insistence, a harassed and overworked staff member again gave him the standard three medications. At a follow-up appointment, however, he learned that he still tested positive for bacteria in his sputum, meaning he was probably infectious with drug-resistant TB. "I been with my kids for a month or more," he worried. "The doc wants them to come in and get tested. There's a chance I infected them."

MYCOBACTERIUM TUBERCULOSIS

Tuberculosis is a chronic or acute infection caused by bacteria that belong to the genus *Mycobacterium*, a group of

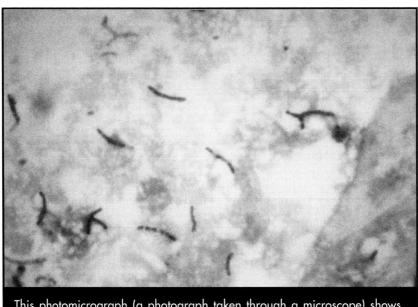

This photomicrograph (a photograph taken through a microscope) shows the *Mycobacterium tuberculosis* bacteria. The bacteria has been dyed to make it easier to see.

rod-shaped organisms that are very small, only 2 to 4 micrometers (0.000079–0.000157 inches) in length. They are known as "acid-fast" bacteria because their cell walls resist acid solutions used in laboratory tests. Early researchers found it impossible to isolate and identify TB bacilli until they understood this characteristic and adopted new testing techniques.

There are over fifty types of mycobacteria. The primary source of TB in humans is *Mycobacterium tuberculosis*, which needs oxygen to live and does not grow in soil or water but can survive outside the human body for many years. Another mycobacterium, *M. bovis*, infects cattle and has been an important source of TB in humans in the past when they ate infected meat or drank infected milk. Routine cattle tests and the pasteurization of milk have removed most of the danger from that source. *M. avium* causes lung disease in poultry and birds and can be a serious source of infection for people with AIDS. One of the most infamous mycobacteria is *M. leprae*, which causes leprosy.

Tuberculosis may be contracted through skin wounds, tattoo procedures, and from mother to child before or during birth, but such cases are rare. The vast majority of the time, TB is transmitted through the air, when a person who is infectious coughs, sneezes, or in some other way expels small droplets of moisture that contain thousands of germs. While the largest of these droplets fall to the ground, smaller ones evaporate and allow TB germs to escape and float about where they can be inhaled by a random passerby. TB bacteria are highly infectious. Only one or two are needed to cause infection under the right conditions.

TB commonly causes disease in the lungs, but bacteria can pass from the lungs into the bloodstream or lymph system and spread to other parts of the body as well. This is called extrapulmonary, or disseminated, tuberculosis and can be very serious if untreated. Young children and persons with AIDS are at the highest risk of developing disseminated

TB. Almost every part of the body can be affected by tuberculosis—the bones and joints, kidneys and bladder, intestines, lymph nodes, skin, eyes, and genital organs.

STAGES OF TUBERCULOSIS

Primary Infection

There are three stages of tuberculosis—primary infection, latent infection, and active disease. Primary infection occurs after a person is exposed to someone with active tuberculosis disease. Tuberculosis bacilli are inhaled, advance through nasal passages, the windpipe, bronchial tubes, and smaller branches of the lungs called bronchioles, all of which are lined with a layer of mucus that traps particles that happen to be passing. Tiny hairlike projections called cilia lie below, and their waving motion produces currents that propel bacteria-ridden mucus upward toward the throat, where it can be swallowed, spit out, or blown into a tissue. Bacteria that evade these defenses and get far enough to lodge in the alveoli (tiny air sacs at the ends of the smallest air passages deep in the lungs) have infected the human host.

Even after bacteria reach the alveoli, the body has further defenses that are powerful and effective. Amoeba-like macrophages—large white blood cells that are part of the body's immune system—attack the invading bacilli, digesting many of them before they can do significant damage. M. *tuberculosis* is protected by a waxy cell wall made up of fatty molecules, however, so many bacteria are able to survive even after they are engulfed by macrophages. Nevertheless, the macrophages do prevent them from migrating to other parts of the body.

Macrophages are joined by T-cells and other white blood cells, which clump together at the site of infection to form a small, hard swelling called a tubercle, or granuloma. In effect, the tubercle acts as a wall to isolate bacteria from the rest of the body. Dying cells inside the tubercle form caseous (soft, cheeselike) areas that support the growth of more bacteria. As the body's immune system continues to battle the bacteria, the tubercle is eventually surrounded by tough scar tissue. Scar tissue cuts off much of the oxygen that *M. tuberculosis* needs to grow. In some cases, all the bacteria die, the tubercle calcifies (hardens), and the host is no longer infected. In other cases, however, bacteria remain alive but inactive inside the tubercles. The host has no symptoms of tuberculosis and is not contagious, although a skin test or a chest X-ray will reveal that he or she has been infected.

Latent Infection
When tuberculosis bacteria remain alive inside a tubercle for years without causing disease, the host is said to have a latent infection. Although infected, he or she remains healthy and symptom free and may never develop disease—only 5 to 10 percent of people with a latent infection will develop TB in their lifetime. Skin tests will show that exposure to tuberculosis bacteria has taken place at some point in time, but many individuals will be surprised by these findings and will wonder when and where they came in contact with an infected person.

If the body's defense mechanisms should ever become weakened due to disease, age, or some other condition, live bacteria inside the tubercle can reactivate and renew their assault on the body. Symptoms will begin to appear, and a doctor will diagnose an active infection. About half of all active cases of TB develop from latent infections that have remained dormant for years within tubercles in the lungs.

Active Disease
Tuberculosis disease develops when bacteria actively replicate in the lungs or in other parts of the body. This may occur shortly after primary infection—as is often the case with children under the age of five, the elderly, and those with impaired immune systems—or much later in a person's lifetime. Half of all active cases of TB stem from infection

that has taken place within the past two years. Damage to tissues results from the host's immune response to an invader (the response of macrophages and other immune cells), not because of toxins produced by the TB bacteria.

No one knows exactly what causes tuberculosis bacteria to reactivate, but the tiny microbes somehow become capable of overpowering the body's immune system. They then burst forth from tubercles and spill out into the lungs, lymph vessels, or bloodstream, where they can be carried to other parts of the body. The bacteria reproduce slowly but vigorously, taking twelve to twenty hours to replicate once. (In contrast, some intestinal bacteria reproduce every twenty minutes.)

Despite this slowness, M. *tuberculosis* can produce significant damage in a relatively short time, generating a nodule (a small, knotlike lump or growth) in the lungs in just ten days and a cavity (a hole in the lung) in a month. While such activity is going on, the patient will show symptoms, will be infectious, and must be isolated to prevent the spread of bacteria to friends, family, and others with whom he has close, continued contact.

SYMPTOMS OF PULMONARY TUBERCULOSIS

Tuberculosis that develops in the lungs is termed pulmonary tuberculosis and is the most common form of the disease. Symptoms of active pulmonary tuberculosis include the following:

- A bad cough that lasts longer than two weeks
- Coughing up sputum or blood
- Pain in the chest
- Weakness or fatigue
- Weight loss
- Loss of appetite
- Chills and fever
- Sweating at night

Coughing and sputum production are two definitive symptoms of pulmonary tuberculosis. The cough may be mild at first, but it does not go away. Patients and doctors sometimes mistake it for an aftereffect of flu or a lingering cold. As the disease progresses, coughing can become extremely severe, and the patient may see blood in the sputum (a condition called hemoptysis), an indication that blood vessels in the lungs have been damaged.

Sputum production is another trademark of TB. When bacteria begin to attack the lungs and white blood cells rush to fight infection, both cells and lung tissue are destroyed. Large amounts of caseous material are continually produced. This cheeselike material liquefies, moves up the respiratory tract, and mixes with saliva to become sputum, which the patient coughs up in copious amounts.

Damage to the lungs and the lining of the lungs may cause the patient to experience chest pain. Sweating at night, the result of subsiding fever, may be heavy, to the extent that night clothes or bedsheets have to be changed. Other symptoms may be troublesome as well. "I had back pain and numbness in my arm," says Sonia, a nurse with the disease. "My doctor seemed to think those were kind of unusual symptoms for TB."

Tuberculosis in children may produce no typical symptoms, so physicians may miss the problem during a checkup. Many children are diagnosed only when health-department workers are examining the contacts of an adult with the disease. "My kids don't act sick," Randall points out. "But the doc says that don't mean nothin'. They might be infected and then get sick real quick. TB can be pretty bad for little kids."

If tuberculosis disease is not treated, the lungs may become so damaged that breathing is very difficult. After what is usually a long, lingering illness that consumes the body, the patient dies, usually from hemorrhage (bleeding) in the lungs. Without treatment, the death rate for untreated cases of TB is 40 to 60 percent.

SYMPTOMS OF
EXTRAPULMONARY TUBERCULOSIS

Tuberculosis that occurs outside the lungs is termed extra-pulmonary tuberculosis and occurs in about 15 percent of all cases. The sites and symptoms of extrapulmonary TB include the following:

Bones and joints. TB bacteria can infect the spine and cause a hunchback condition termed Pott's disease. The ends of the long bones of the arms and legs can also be affected, resulting in pain and paralysis if not treated. Tuberculosis of the joints can lead to tuberculous arthritis. Weight-bearing joints such as knees and hips are most often affected, but wrists, hands, and elbows may also suffer.

Kidney and bladder. Infection causes destruction of tissue but produces few early symptoms.

Intestines. Tuberculosis of the intestines can be asymptomatic (causing no symptoms), or it can be very painful. It may produce a tumor in the infected area that can be mistaken for cancer.

Lymph nodes. Infected lymph nodes in the neck can become enlarged and may break through the skin and discharge pus, a condition traditionally known as scrofula. In children, nodes can enlarge to such an extent that they compress the bronchial tubes, producing a brassy cough and sometimes a collapsed lung.

Skin. Tuberculosis of the skin causes inflammation, pain, rashes, and lesions.

Genital organs. Infection of genital organs may cause tumors, scarring, and sterility.

Brain and spinal cord. This infection is termed tuberculous meningitis. The condition is extremely dangerous, progresses rapidly, and usually causes death without proper treatment. Symptoms include high fever, intense headache, nausea, stiff neck, and drowsiness that can lead to coma.

Miliary tuberculosis. Miliary TB is an acute form of the disease that occurs when a large number of bacteria spread by way of the bloodstream to every organ in the body. The condition is marked by tiny nodules about the size of a grain of millet (birdseed). Symptoms are often vague and hard to identify. They may include high fever, chills, difficulty breathing, general discomfort, severe anemia, and other blood abnormalities. Miliary tuberculosis is one of the most deadly forms of TB.

FURTHER COMPLICATIONS

The symptoms of tuberculosis have been well documented and well known for years, and health-care workers have the knowledge and skill to recognize the many manifestations of the disease, whether it occurs in bones, lymph nodes, or other parts of the body. In recent years, however, further complications have arisen in connection with TB, adding to its complexity as well as its lethal potential. Two of the most serious of those complications are AIDS and drug resistance.

TUBERCULOSIS AND AIDS

One of the foremost causes of the upswing in tuberculosis cases in recent times is HIV, which destroys the immune system, leads to AIDS, and allows disease to wreck havoc with a victim's health. Tuberculosis is one of the most common infections to plague people living with AIDS. One-third of the forty million people with AIDS worldwide also have TB, and tuberculosis is one of the leading causes of death among people with AIDS.

Symptoms of active tuberculosis in a person with AIDS are much the same as for persons without AIDS—coughing, sputum production, weight loss, and fever—but in AIDS patients, these can be masked by other opportunistic infections that have similar symptoms. For instance, infection by the *Pneumocystis carinii* fungus produces pneumonia-like symptoms. Infection by the

Histoplasma capsulatum fungus causes weight loss, fever, and respiratory complications.

When combined, HIV and TB are particularly deadly in that they appear to activate each other. That is, tuberculosis seems to have the ability to accelerate the course of an individual's HIV infection, triggering a full-blown case of AIDS. Conversely, a person with HIV or AIDS is more liable to catch tuberculosis, more likely to develop the disease soon after infection, and more likely to go from latent to active TB within months of an HIV infection.

One example of this increased susceptibility involved a prison in South Carolina. In November 1998, the prison began moving inmates with AIDS into a special dormitory within the prison. In August 1999, one of the inmates was diagnosed with TB, and the other inmates were subsequently tested. Of the more than three hundred inmates in the dormitory, thirty-one had contracted TB from this one infected individual. Ordinarily, it would take many years for a single case to infect so many people.

DRUG-RESISTANT TUBERCULOSIS

The growing incidence of drug-resistant strains of tuberculosis bacteria is another complication that has TB experts on the alert. Decades ago, doctors observed that *M. tuberculosis* became unresponsive to antibiotics after only a short period of treatment, although no one understood the mechanism by which this was able to occur.

As studies progressed, researchers learned that living cells sometimes mutate—randomly alter their genetic makeup—during the process of division, producing physical or functional changes. For instance, a bacterium might contain a specific site on its cell wall where an antibiotic would normally attach and disable it. If, however, the bacterium mutated so that the site changed or disappeared, the antibiotic was no longer able to attack. The bacterium was said to have developed resistance to that particular drug. And because the mutation involved a change in genetic material, it was passed along every time the bacterium reproduced itself. Thus, all offspring of the original bacterium were drug resistant. Such is the case of *M. tuberculosis*, which has proven particularly adept at changing its genetic makeup again and again over time in order to protect itself and survive.

Drug resistance is a very real problem in the treatment of tuberculosis. The duration of treatment for the disease is quite long, giving the bacteria plenty of time to mutate and develop resistance. Doctors and health officials have sometimes contributed to the problem by prescribing drugs incorrectly and by discontinuing treatment before a patient is fully cured. Some patients make things worse by carelessness and irresponsibility. Most of these are not hospitalized during treatment and so have no one to supervise and ensure the correct taking of medicines. Those who are homeless, addicted to drugs, or just plain careless fail to take every type of medication prescribed or do not take their full course of medication and thus end up with strains of the disease that can be resistant to several antibiotics.

Randall is a case in point. When he repeatedly stopped taking his medication, convinced that he was cured because his cough and fever had disappeared, he had only temporarily curbed the disease by eliminating the weakest bacteria from his system. Those germs that remained in his lungs were those that were more resistant to antibiotics. Doctors who tried to convince him of the importance of taking each and every dose of medication to ensure that the bacteria were truly eliminated found him skeptical. "They say 'take the pills for a year and you'll be well,' but I'll probably never be well again," he says. "Why should I take a bunch of pills that make me feel even worse? It don't make sense."

When drug-resistant tuberculosis first appeared on the health scene, experts hoped that such strains would be weak and incapable of infecting other people. This has not proved to be the case, however. Drug-resistant strains of TB are less capable of infection than nonresistant strains, but there are still approximately 450,000 new cases of drug-resistant TB each year. Increasing numbers of people are coming down with tough-to-cure infections, despite the fact that they take their medicine correctly. In one study of almost 500 patients in New York City, 70 percent of them had multidrug-resistant TB when their infection was first identified—that is, their disease was resistant to two or more antitubercular antibiotics from the start. These patients were often health-care workers who contracted the disease from individuals with resistant strains of TB. The resistant strains were passed through the air, just as ordinary strains have always been.

Up to fifty million people worldwide are infected with drug-resistant strains of tuberculosis. Drug-resistant TB has been diagnosed in over forty states in the United States and in at least thirty-five countries worldwide. Those individuals who are at highest risk for developing drug-resistant TB include:

- Those who have spent time with someone with drug-resistant TB
- Patients with TB who do not take their medications regularly or who do not take all of their medicine
- Those who develop resistant TB disease after having taken TB medication in the past
- Individuals from areas where drug-resistant TB is common, such as Southeast Asia, Latin America, Haiti, and the Philippines

In countries with high rates of resistant tuberculosis, about one-third of all TB cases are virtually incurable. Some strains have been found that are resistant to as many as seven antibiotics. One has been found that is resistant to eleven. In the United States, the greatest danger appears to be in New York City, where approximately one-third of the nation's multidrug-resistant cases since 1993 have occurred. "We have turned a disease that was completely preventable and curable into one that is neither," says Dr. Lee Reichman, one of the leading tuberculosis experts in the United States and past president of the American Lung Association. "We should be ashamed."

An outbreak of multidrug-resistant TB in South Africa beginning in May 2005 has been especially deadly due to the high rates of HIV in that country. More than 85 percent of South Africans with HIV and this strain of TB have died. A slow government response allowed the disease to spread to all of South Africa's provinces and most likely to nearby countries as well.

Whether tuberculosis is susceptible to drug therapy, manifests itself as a complication of AIDS, or mutates into resistant strains, medical officials need the best and most up-to-date methods of detection and treatment in order to curb its potentially deadly force. After years of neglecting the disease, they are only beginning to make progress in this area. The means by which tuberculosis is diagnosed and treated is explored more fully in chapter 4.

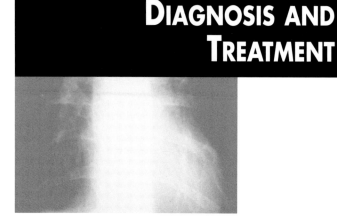

DIAGNOSIS AND TREATMENT

Sonia's Story

Sonia and her parents came to the United States from Ukraine in 1993, two years after the fall of Communism in the Soviet Union. The economy of Ukraine was in decline, money was tight, and the future uncertain. When relatives in Chicago suggested that the family begin a new life in the United States, Sonia and her parents eagerly made the move.

In hopes of contributing something positive to her community and her new country, Sonia became a practical nurse after graduation from high school. She was hired to work in a nursing home and obediently took the TB skin test that was required of all employees. The test came back positive. Sonia explained that she had lived for a time with her grandmother who had had tuberculosis but that she had also received a TB vaccine as part of a mandatory governmental health program when she was a child. The vaccine was supposed to give measured protection against TB and always caused the one immunized to react to a skin test. Sonia's supervisor made a note of the fact and allowed her to begin work without further ado.

During her second year on the job, Sonia developed what appeared to be a bad cold and an annoying cough that would not go away. Her family doctor first prescribed cough syrup and then diagnosed asthma and gave her an inhaler, which she used conscientiously. Despite ill health, she continued to go to work every day. "I even kept my sessions at the gym, thinking the exercise would make me feel better," she explains. "Aerobics classes made the coughing and back pain worse, so I just concentrated on the treadmill and easy stuff on the weight machines."

Finally, Sonia's supervisor at work insisted that she go back to the doctor. There had been several cases of tuberculosis among the patients in the nursing home in the past few years, and some of the staff now tested positive for exposure to the disease. Sonia's vaccination, of course, invalidated any skin-test results, but her symptoms seemed ominous. When she mentioned her possible exposure to TB, her doctor ordered chest X-rays. "I guess I wasn't surprised when he broke the news," she said. "It was TB—I had a pretty big hole in my left lung. The doctor was astounded that I'd had the strength to keep up my exercise routine, as sick as I was."

Sonia was treated with a standard combination of antibiotics, but tests still showed signs of an active infection several weeks later. Other antibiotic combinations proved just as ineffective, and her health continued to deteriorate. She lost weight and coughed up blood. She had surgery to drain fluid from her lung. "It was the most terrible time in my life," she said. "My family and friends hardly dared come and visit me. I couldn't leave my room. No one said so, but I knew I was dying."

Sonia's physician finally referred her to National Jewish Medical and Research Center in Denver, Colorado, one of the world's foremost TB hospitals and the last hope for many extremely sick tubercular patients. At National Jewish, doctors determined that radical treatments were necessary and set about doing what they could to save Sonia's disease-ravaged lungs.

PREVENTING TUBERCULOSIS

The Bacillus Calmette-Guerin Vaccine

Antibiotic treatment is the standard means of controlling and curing most cases of tuberculosis, but many governments throughout the world seek to prevent outbreaks of the disease by use of the Bacillus Calmette-Guerin (BCG) vaccine developed by researchers Albert Calmette and Camille Guerin at the Pasteur Institute in Lille, France, between 1908 and 1921. Made from live weakened *M. bovis*, the vaccine does not prevent infection but has proven effective in preventing the development of TB disease in children. At the recommendation of the World Health Organization (WHO), BCG is given to up to 8 percent of the world's infants as part of their immunization program.

Despite its widespread use, BCG has many shortcomings and remains controversial, particularly in the United States. The protection it gives is highly variable, perhaps because there is no standardized technique for making the vaccine. Resistance to TB may last for many years, for a relatively short time, or not at all. In one study, infection appeared to be higher in the group who received BCG than in control groups who did not. "It is puzzling that BCG's protective efficacy against pulmonary tuberculosis in adults has varied from zero to 77 percent in different studies," says Dr. Barry Bloom, a consultant to the World Health Organization.

Once a person is vaccinated with BCG, a tuberculin skin test, the most common means of diagnosing recent infection, becomes useless. Throughout a lifetime, an immunized individual will have a positive reaction, indicating that he or she has been exposed to the bacteria through the vaccine. Such a result would be a negligible problem if BCG gave lifetime protection against TB. The vaccine's variable protection, however, leaves health-care workers wondering if a person is newly infected or whether he or she is simply reacting to BCG.

A third problem with the BCG vaccine is that some doctors hesitate to give it to individuals with weakened immune systems (such as those infected with HIV) who could most benefit from protection. Because the vaccine is made of live bacteria, there are fears that it could cause tuberculosis disease in such individuals, although studies carried out in Africa and Asia seem to disprove that possibility.

U.S. health officials oppose the widespread use of BCG, particularly in countries where rates of tuberculosis are low, but they recognize the value of preventive treatment to control tuberculosis. Thus, they emphasize the need for development of new, more effective vaccines that will finally bring an end to disputes over whether or not to use BCG. In the early twenty-first century, several new vaccines for TB are being tested across the globe.

Preventive Antibiotic Therapy

If a person is exposed to someone with active tuberculosis, or if a skin test indicates that a person has been infected with *M. tuberculosis*, a physician often prescribes the antibiotic isoniazid to prevent infection from developing into active disease. Isoniazid therapy must continue for six months or as long as a physician indicates in order for it to be fully effective.

Children under five years old can develop tuberculous meningitis in as little as six weeks after infection and thus should begin isoniazid treatment even if a skin test is negative. If a follow-up skin test remains negative, treatment can be discontinued. Otherwise, it should continue for nine months.

HIV-infected patients who are infected with TB should be treated with isoniazid for twelve months. When health officials determine that an individual has been infected with TB strains resistant to isoniazid, treatment involves a different medication such as rifampicin.

DIAGNOSING TUBERCULOSIS

The Mantoux Skin Test

The most common method of testing a person for infection by *M. tuberculosis* is the tuberculin skin test. The test involves injecting a small amount of liquid filtered from weakened, nonvirulent tubercle bacillus (termed purified protein derivative, or PPD) under the skin of the forearm or administering it with a multipronged device. The former is known as the Mantoux test and is preferred because there is no way to be sure that an adequate amount of PPD is being injected in the latter procedure.

The skin test is based on the body's immune response to infection. When initially infected by a foreign substance, the body reacts by forming antibodies, protein molecules that act as defense against attack. Characteristic symptoms of reaction include pain, swelling, and reddening at the site of infection. Antibodies remain long after infection occurs, and reinfection by the same foreign substance will spark a similar reaction—such is the case with a skin test if a person has been previously infected with TB. A red welt appears on the arm within seventy-two hours, indicating a positive reaction to the injected bacterial protein, and signifying that TB infection has probably occurred sometime in the past.

False positive results can occur if a person has been vaccinated with the BCG vaccine or exposed to bacteria related to M. *tuberculosis*. False negatives can occur if an individual has a weakened immune system or if the test is administered too soon after exposure to M. *tuberculosis*. It takes up to three months after being infected with tuberculosis for the body to produce antibodies and for a skin test to be positive.

"Both Mica and Denise had a negative skin reaction when they were tested," David explains. "I guess that signified that exposure had taken place within just the last couple of months—to me, of course. Since Mica was already very sick, the doctor went ahead and did lab tests

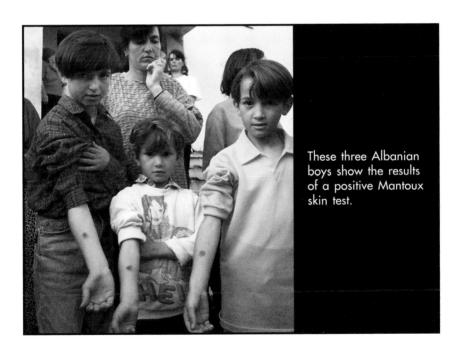

These three Albanian boys show the results of a positive Mantoux skin test.

and got her started on antibiotics. According to him, it's fairly typical for little kids to get sick with TB before the test shows they've even been exposed. That's one of the dangers of this old disease."

Who Should Have a Skin Test?

Everyone should have a skin test at least once in order to know whether they have a negative or positive reaction for tuberculosis. Others who should be tested at regular intervals after that include:

- Those who think they may have been recently exposed to tuberculosis
- Persons with HIV, people with medical conditions such as diabetes or silicosis, and others with compromised immune systems
- People in or from countries where TB disease is common
- People who are residents or who work in long-term facilities such as nursing homes, correctional facilities, or substance abuse centers
- People who work in schools, food-handling establishments, or child care facilities
- People who are underweight
- Alcoholics and persons who inject drugs
- All health-care workers

A skin test can reliably show if a person has been infected with tuberculosis, but it cannot tell if that person has active disease or not. Other tests, such as the chest X-ray and the sputum test, must be administered in order to make that determination.

Chest X-ray

If a person has a positive reaction to a skin test, a doctor will usually order a chest X-ray to help determine if that person has active pulmonary tuberculosis. An X-ray can show evidence of cavities or lesions in the lungs. Such lesions show up as irregular white areas termed shadows against a normally dark background.

X-rays were the accidental discovery of the German physicist Wilhelm K. Roentgen. In 1895, while studying the phenomena of electric discharge, Roentgen discovered rays that were able to penetrate cardboard and produce a black line on specially treated paper. Roentgen called his discovery X-rays because he did not understand what they were. (X is a scientific symbol for the unknown.) The discovery was at first scorned by physicians but soon became widely accepted as a means of diagnosing disease. X-rays proved valuable in diagnosing tuberculosis of the lungs long before a patient began to show symptoms of the disease.

In the 1940s and 1950s, X-rays were used to screen enormous numbers of people for TB, but X-rays soon

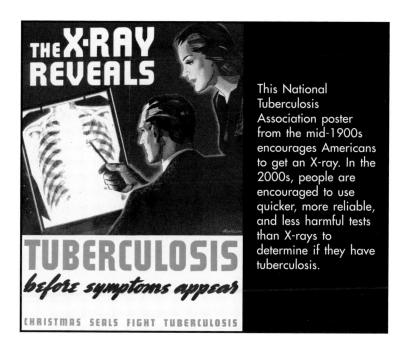

This National Tuberculosis Association poster from the mid-1900s encourages Americans to get an X-ray. In the 2000s, people are encouraged to use quicker, more reliable, and less harmful tests than X-rays to determine if they have tuberculosis.

proved to have their shortcomings. First, repeated use increased an individual's risk of cancer. Next, small tubercular lesions could not be detected in an X-ray, and lesions that appeared to be healed could not be examined for living bacilli. Finally, physicians could not determine with certainty if abnormalities of the lungs were caused by tuberculosis or some other lung disease such as cancer or a fungus infection. Today, X-rays are still used as part of a TB diagnosis, but new diagnostic techniques are being developed that promise to give reliable results more quickly and efficiently than more traditional diagnostic methods.

Laboratory Tests

To confirm the presence of active tuberculosis in an individual and to learn about the bacterial strain with which they are dealing, doctors rely on laboratory tests, which are more informative than skin tests and X-rays. A smear of sputum or mucus (or if extrapulmonary TB is suspected, a sample of spinal fluid, urine, or tissue) is obtained, placed on a slide, stained with chemicals, and observed under a microscope. Next, the sample is cultured—that is, a smear is placed in a petri dish or test tube and allowed to grow for a period of time. Since tuberculosis bacteria reproduce so slowly, it sometimes takes a month to grow enough to verify the bacteria's identity and weeks or months after that to determine if those bacteria are resistant to one or more antibiotics.

Severely ill patients—particularly those with AIDS, whose disease progresses rapidly—can die in the time it takes to culture their bacteria, so new techniques that can accelerate diagnosis are welcomed by health workers. One such technique, used in a growing number of cases, is the polymerase chain reaction (PCR) developed in 1992. PCR uses a segment of bacterial DNA to produce millions of copies of genetic material, which can then be analyzed and identified. Although originally a difficult and expensive process that could only be performed in laboratories, it has since been simplified and can be performed at most clinics in the twenty-first century.

TREATING TUBERCULOSIS

Antitubercular Medications

Treatment for tuberculosis requires chemotherapy—use of chemical agents or drugs—and involves taking a variety of powerful antibiotics until all bacteria are destroyed. The most common antibiotics used to fight tuberculosis in the twenty-first century are:

Isoniazid. One of the most effective antitubercular drugs, isoniazid is also used to prevent active disease from developing. It kills almost all mycobacteria.

Rifampicin. A derivative of the antibiotic rifamycin, rifampicin is, like isoniazid, bactericidal (a bacteria killer).

Rifabutin. A modified form of rifampicin, rifabutin can be taken in smaller doses, penetrates better into diseased tissues, and remains active longer than its precursor.

Pyrazinamide. Commonly used in combination with isoniazid and rifampicin, pyrazinamide appears to kill bacteria that survive within macrophages.

Ethambutol. Inhibits but does not kill bacteria effectively. Ethambutol is not recommended for children under the age of eight, since it can impair vision and its effects are difficult to monitor.

Streptomycin. The first antibiotic to be developed and used against tuberculosis, streptomycin is bactericidal. It is now used primarily for advanced or resistant infections. Streptomycin can affect a person's balance and hearing if it is administered for longer than three months.

Standard Therapy for TB Disease

When a person has active tuberculosis, he or she is highly infectious and is usually hospitalized for a time, depending on the severity of the disease and how quickly it responds to treatment. "I stayed in the hospital while they did tests," sixteen-year-old Jodi explains. "Once I got on medications and began feeling better, the doctor let me go home to finish my treatment there. It was all pretty routine, unless you count my pee turning orange from one of the drugs. That was kind of scary. Otherwise, I just hung around, stayed home from school, and stayed away from my friends until I was germ-free. It wasn't too bad."

Antibiotic treatment is highly effective if it is administered and taken properly. Although 40 to 60 percent of untreated patients die of tuberculosis, more than 90 percent can be cured by proper antibiotic therapy. (These figures do not include persons with drug-resistant strains.) Treatment options involve frequent dosages of medication, and proper therapy always requires taking three to four drugs at the same time to counter drug resistance. Patients with drug-susceptible TB (pulmonary and extrapulmonary) are commonly given rifampicin, isoniazid, and pyrazinamide daily for two months, followed by isoniazid and rifampicin daily or twice weekly for at least four additional months. In the United States, rifampicin, isoniazid, and pyrazinamide are now available in the same capsule, marketed under the name Rifater. This combined medication reduces the number of pills a person has to take each day and helps ensure that all necessary medication is taken.

Treatment for tuberculosis is lengthy—six months is usually the minimum time needed for antibiotics to totally eliminate all TB bacteria in a patient's lungs and lymph nodes—but patients are usually not infectious after just a few weeks of medication, and outpatient care is the norm. Physicians usually allow patients to return home and to a normal routine as long as they continue to take their medicine. Treatment of TB of the joints and bones requires a longer term of therapy, as does treatment of miliary TB and tuberculous meningitis.

Side Effects

Since drugs that weaken and destroy tuberculosis bacteria are powerful, side effects are common. Minor side effects include: orange urine, saliva, and/or tears; sensitivity of the skin to the sun; and ineffectiveness of birth control pills and implants.

If side effects are more serious, the patient should consult his doctor so that a substitute drug can be prescribed. Serious side effects can include loss of appetite, nausea, vomiting, abdominal pain, dizziness, easy bruising, skin rash, aching joints, hearing loss, yellowish skin or eyes, fever lasting three or more days, tingling of the fingers or toes, tingling or numbness around the mouth, blurred or changed vision, ringing in the ears, and personality changes.

Incomplete Treatment

As a patient begins to feel better, he or she may decide that the side effects of the drug are more unpleasant than the disease itself. TB bacteria are still alive in the body, however, and will rebound if treatment is discontinued. Serious complications that can arise if TB medications are not taken as prescribed include: bacteria becoming resistant to one or more of the drugs, an increased risk of toxic reactions from the drugs, and a high risk of relapse and recurrence of active disease.

TREATMENT OF MULTIDRUG-RESISTANT TUBERCULOSIS

A patient needs to be regularly monitored by a doctor during treatment of tuberculosis to determine if a strain of bacteria is susceptible or resistant to antibiotics. An individual may be displaying signs of drug resistance if:

- Symptoms do not improve during the first two months of treatment or worsen after initial improvement

- Sputum tests are not clear of bacteria after two months
- Sputum tests that have tested clear of bacteria again show evidence of bacteria

When drug resistance occurs, adjustments in treatment are necessary for the patient to recover. Physicians—preferably specialists who understand how to manage the disease—must go to greater lengths to bring about a cure, and despite their best efforts, they are sometimes unsuccessful. Less than 50 percent of patients with resistant strains of tuberculosis recover with treatment, compared to over 90 percent of patients with nonresistant strains.

Because of the contagiousness and tenacity of resistant infections, initial treatment should always take place in a hospital setting. There the patient can be monitored for progress and for side effects of the large doses of drugs needed to fight the disease. Therapy is as grueling as cancer chemotherapy, and can be an extremely lonely experience because patients must remain isolated. It includes taking at least four antibiotics concurrently, and at least two of these must kill rather than simply inhibit bacterial growth. Difficulty sometimes arises in finding antibiotics to which resistant bacteria respond. In order to weaken bacteria and allow the body to fight the disease, doctors must continually adjust dosages and sometimes turn to medicines that are not as effective or that have highly undesirable side effects such as personality changes and psychosis.

"The great majority of our patients who are being intensively treated suffer from continuous adverse side effects from their medicines," says Dr. Michael Iseman, a top TB specialist at National Jewish Medical and Research Center in Denver, Colorado. The sickest patients sometimes take as many as sixteen pills daily and a series of shots several times a week to suppress infection. Treatment often lasts for two years rather than the six to eighteen months needed for standard treatment.

SURGICAL THERAPY

When tuberculosis proves resistant to all known antibiotics and the prognosis for the patient is death, doctors who are experts in the field may go to extreme lengths in a final effort to effect a cure.

At National Jewish Medical and Research Center, surgical procedures invented early in the twentieth century are used to save some of the sickest tuberculosis patients. Utilizing a procedure called pneumothorax, air is pumped into the chest or abdominal cavity, effectively collapsing a diseased lung and eliminating pockets where bacteria can survive. Another technique involves temporary inactivation of the nerve that runs to the diaphragm, the muscular wall that divides the chest cavity from the abdominal cavity. With the nerve disabled, the diaphragm moves upward into the chest region, again helping to collapse a diseased lung. (The nerve regenerates in about six months.)

In some cases, a pneumonectomy, or pulmonary resection, is performed. In that procedure, doctors remove severely damaged portions of a lung, taking with them large numbers of bacteria. The strongest antibiotics are then prescribed to get rid of remaining infection. "We are willing to gamble on very painful and risky treatments because this is [a patient's] last shot," says Iseman. "If we can't control their disease, they die the death of consumption, slowly strangled as the TB eats away at their lungs."

THERAPY FOR AIDS-RELATED TB

Diagnosing TB in HIV-infected individuals can be difficult. They may have other conditions that produce symptoms similar to those of TB. Those with AIDS may not react to a tuberculin skin test (their immune systems are suppressed), so they need to be tested by other means and monitored carefully for infection.

Prevention of the development of TB is a top priority among persons with HIV or AIDS. All who have been exposed to TB need to be placed on isoniazid preventive therapy. New multidrug preventive regimes that include rifamycin combined with pyrazinamide are also proving effective.

Treatment for active TB disease in HIV or AIDS patients is most effective if it is started as early as possible, so as to counteract the two diseases' ability to stimulate each other. AIDS patients often require repeated courses of chemotherapy to keep TB disease under control. The longer they are on such treatment, however, the more chances their bacteria have to develop resistance to antibiotics. Even with treatment, the death rate for those with multidrug-resistant TB and AIDS can be as high as 80 percent.

Because many HIV and AIDS patients are infected with multidrug-resistant tuberculosis and many AIDS-related TB infections are slow to respond to treatment, some doctors are now treating every infection of this type as if it were drug resistant. Treatment usually follows along the lines of multidrug-resistant chemotherapy. Unfortunately, certain drugs developed to treat HIV and AIDS interact with rifampicin, reducing the effectiveness of both types of treatment. Substitution of rifabutin for rifampicin allows patients to continue protease inhibitor therapy while they are being treated for TB.

INCENTIVE PROGRAMS

Convincing patients to take their medicine for the entire time needed to eliminate infection is the biggest problem doctors and health workers face in the fight against tuberculosis. In 1992 officials estimated that 40 percent of TB patients in New York City stopped taking their medications too soon. One New York City hospital discovered that almost 90 percent of their TB patients failed to complete treatment. The result was incomplete recovery and more cases of drug-resistant disease.

Many patients who fail to complete prescribed treatment are like Randall—homeless, addicted to drugs and alcohol, suspicious of authorities, or ignorant of the terrible threat they pose to society when they do not take medications properly. Health officials despair when patients fail to return to clinics for follow-up appointments or return to say that they have stopped taking their pills because of the side effects.

To combat the problem, some cities have created incentive programs in the hope of gaining patients' cooperation. Some programs give free lunches or subway tokens to those who come in to get their medicines. Others reward cooperation with fast-food coupons, a free night's lodging, or personal items, plus a cash bonus for finishing treatment on time. Such programs have proved highly successful. Since 1994 more than 90 percent of patients in New York completed their treatment.

DIRECTLY OBSERVED THERAPY, SHORT-COURSE

Incentive programs work, but health officials have determined that direct supervision of patients is the most certain and effective way to ensure that they take their medicine for the full course of treatment. To that end, the World Health Organization endorses a strategy termed Directly Observed Therapy, Short-Course (DOTS), that relies on closely supervised treatment programs to help control and eliminate tuberculosis around the world. With DOTS, national or local governments comply with WHO guidelines in the following ways: Cases of active TB are detected and reported by health departments and other health organizations, and medications are provided; field-workers and trained volunteers watch patients take each and every one of their pills for the entire course of treatment; and patients' progress is recorded and reported. Ideally, health-care workers meet patients at prearranged spots to carry out their supervisory tasks. The job is often more complicated, however, with workers expending much time and energy tracking down the patient to a new job, a friend's home, or even a crack house and then relying on arguments and ingenuity to convince the person to take the daily medication.

A DOTS tuberculosis patient in Durban, South Africa, shows her health worker that she has swallowed her pill.

DOTS programs require much time and commitment, but they work. Cure rates of up to 95 percent have been reported even in the poorest countries. In parts of China, DOTS has produced 96 percent cure rates among new cases, and in Peru, use of DOTS for more than five years has led to successful treatment of over 90 percent of cases and a decline in overall numbers of infection. In New York

City, new cases of TB went down by 65 percent between 1993 and 2004, largely due to DOTS. Drug resistant cases fell over 90 percent.

According to the United Nations-sponsored World Bank, which helps finance projects for developing nations, DOTS is one of the most cost-effective health intervention programs in the world. A six-month supply of drugs needed to cure TB costs only about eleven dollars per patient in many countries. In addition, millions of dollars in treatment are being saved despite the initial investment of hiring a large number of health workers to supervise treatments. Patients are recovering more quickly, and fewer expensive-to-treat drug-resistant strains have a chance to develop.

DETENTION

Perhaps the most controversial treatment to have been implemented in the United States is detention—locking up tuberculosis patients who are infectious and refuse to take their medicine. Detainees are usually those who have been treated for TB at least three times in the past and continue to refuse or fail to complete treatment. In some cities, those individuals are picked up by the police, placed under guard in isolation rooms in hospitals or prison infirmaries, and literally forced to take prescribed medicines until they are noninfectious or cured.

New York City implemented a detention program in 1993, primarily because so many of the city's uncooperative patients had drug-resistant strains and were spreading infections that were difficult if not impossible to cure. Similar programs have also been set up in Colorado, California, and Massachusetts.

Results have been positive. On follow-up evaluations, more than three-quarters of those who were detained appeared to be cured and no longer needed to be detained. (The rest had died of other diseases, usually associated with

AIDS, or had moved and could not be located.) The cost of locking up people is much higher than treating them through DOTS programs, so budget-aware officials are using detention only as a last resort. Detention also raises controversy about the rights of individuals. As the rates of TB decline in the United States, detention is rarely used.

As the tuberculosis epidemic in the United States has slowed, detention has been used less frequently. A combination of fewer overall cases of TB and more patients completing their treatment means that it is no longer necessary to detain people nearly as often as it was during the 1990s. However, in certain special cases—where a patient has extensively drug-resistant TB and refuses to cooperate, for example—detention may still be used in order to prevent a

In 2007 CDC director Julie Louise Gerberding appeared before a U.S. Senate subcommittee to answer questions about flawed security and the CDC's role in the Andrew Speaker case.

public-health crisis. Andrew Speaker, whose case was discussed in chapter 2, was put in involuntary isolation upon his return to the United States after his wedding in Greece.

Balancing civil liberties against public health is only one of the dilemmas health officials and government leaders face as they work to combat today's TB epidemic. Other issues, including the growing cost of treatment, impairment of the workforce, and the increased threat to children are just as serious and just as difficult to resolve. These and other challenges society must face will be discussed in depth in chapter 5.

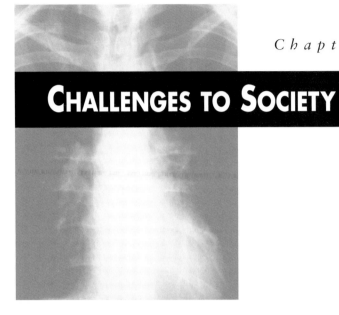

Chapter 5

CHALLENGES TO SOCIETY

Jodi's Story

Jodi lives in a middle-class neighborhood in South-ern California. She is neither poor, malnourished, nor an immigrant. Her family is stable, hardwork-ing, and has good health insurance. Other than her youth, Jodi's only risk factors for catching TB are past family vacations to exotic locales and regular contact with minority students at school, many of whom are relatively recent immigrants from South-east Asia.

Recently, however, Jodi came down with tuber-culosis. Her symptoms first appeared to be like flu that turned into bronchitis. The severity of Jodi's coughing spells frightened her mother, who took her daughter to their family physician. Not in the habit of checking for tuberculosis in patients like

Jodi, the doctor prescribed cough syrup and decongestants and sent her home to rest. Jodi's suffering might have been prolonged if not for further developments: Another mother called the school to report that her daughter was in the hospital with tuberculosis. "One of my friends called to tell me," Jodi explains. "We both knew the girl who was sick. Anyway, the school made the case into a big-deal thing—I guess it had to. Everyone in the student body had to be tested. Anyone who was sick had to go to the doctor."

Jodi and her parents returned to their physician, who admitted Jodi to the hospital. Tests identified her ailment as tuberculosis. "We were stunned," her father admits. "TB was a thing of the past, something my parents talked about. It was just inconceivable that Jodi should have it."

Jodi was started on antibiotic therapy, and her parents were given preventive treatment. Meanwhile, authorities at the school checked teachers and other students for signs of infection or illness. Twelve students—some of whom Jodi knew only by sight—had a positive reaction to a skin test, making it unlikely that she had been the primary source of the outbreak. Three students were ill with what their doctors had previously dismissed as asthma or a virus.

Dr. Richard Jackson, formerly of the Centers for Disease Control and Prevention, points out that schools—high schools in particular—should not be considered unusual settings for a TB epidemic. "High school kids are face to face much more often than other groups," he says. "They sing in choir and shout in class. There is much more talking than in other officelike environments." Although very young children with TB are usually not contagious, teens are fully capable of infecting one another, as Jodi's case indicates.

UNEXPECTED IMPACT

Outbreaks of tuberculosis among ordinary middle-class citizens have been wake-up calls to parents, administrators, and health officials who are not used to seeing TB in stable, healthy populations, and thus have overlooked the potential danger to such groups. "Tuberculosis has come home to roost with a vengeance, and not only among the poor or those with immune deficiencies, but among those in places that have always been considered safe havens, such as sunny open-air California high schools," says Jackson.

Many countries—the United States among them—are now working hard to lower the risk, but not every country is as committed. In the late 1990s, the World Health Organization found that many nations with high tuberculosis rates were among the least compliant with WHO's guidelines for dealing with the disease and were making slow progress in controlling it. Some fell short in uncovering new infections. Some dealt ineffectively with patients who broke off treatment. Some failed to set aside adequate funds to maintain treatment programs. Some failed to report results, a clue that established DOTS programs were deteriorating. Such neglect not only negatively impacts problem countries, but it puts other populations at risk as international travel continues to increase.

Some of the risks and challenges the world faces if tuberculosis is not controlled include:

- Increased infection of the general population
- Greater risk for children
- Loss of life
- Loss of productivity
- Loss of talent in health-related fields
- Growing health costs

Increased Infection of the General Population

Increasing numbers of cases of tuberculosis around the world alarm health officials. They know that the disease will threaten more otherwise healthy individuals if it is allowed to go unchecked. One contagious individual in a classroom, at a workplace, or on an airplane can pass infection to those who would otherwise be at very low risk for catching TB.

The emergence of highly infectious strains of tuberculosis in some locales adds to health officials' worries. In such cases, widespread infection occurs after very short periods of exposure. In a two-year period in Tennessee and Kentucky, for instance, three men passed tuberculosis to more than 72 percent of the people with whom they interacted. Some of their contacts became

If you are an Asian American woman...

LUNG DISEASE DISCRIMINATES

Lung cancer is the third most common cancer among Asian American women.

Three ways that you can help: Educate, Donate, Volunteer.

American Lung Association
Lung Disease Data in
Culturally Diverse Communities 2004.
www.lungusa.org
or call 1-800-LUNGUSA

AMERICAN LUNG ASSOCIATION
100 YEARS • 1904-2004

Improving Life, One Br

This American Lung Association poster warns that TB has a higher rate of occurrence among Asian Americans than among any other ethnic group in the United States.

infected after short get-togethers in the open air, conditions which would normally have been considered low risk. "We've seen transmission occur with minimum contact," says Dr. Sarah Valway, who investigated the outbreak for the Centers for Disease Control and Prevention. "[The contact was] described as hanging outside at the local gas station or outside at night at the Dairy Queen."

If strains such as these become more common, the threat to the general population will rise dramatically. Consequences could be tragic in terms of loss of life.

Greater Risk for Children

Cases of TB among otherwise healthy children and teens are particularly disturbing and serve to emphasize the vulnerability of youth to tuberculosis infection. "It's awful to have to watch your child hurting, particularly when it's from a disease that could have been prevented," Jodi's father says. "We should be doing better by our kids these days."

Children who are infected and/or who develop tuberculosis are significant to health officials because this usually indicates that someone close to the child—a parent or friend—has active TB. A child's age makes it impossible for his or her case to be a result of a long-standing latent infection. Thus, a case of juvenile tuberculosis is an alarm bell for health officials, who must track down the source of the infection and then identify others whom that person may have infected. The task is time consuming but necessary if the public's health is to be protected. Dr. Dixie E. Snider, formerly with the CDC points out, "The continuing occurrence of tuberculosis in children is a sentinel health event—a warning signal that the quality of medical care needs to be improved."

While not every child who is exposed will develop active tuberculosis, those who are unaware that they have been infected prolong the TB threat to society in the future. "I could have been infected with TB when I was a kid, I don't know," says David. "I could feel guilty that I didn't do something to prevent getting sick, but how can you fix something you don't know you have? There must be thousands—millions—of people out there like me. Ticking TB time bombs, waiting to go off."

Loss of Life

Nearly two million people globally die annually from tuberculosis, and that number appears likely to increase in the future. The vast majority of the world's fifteen million active cases of TB are in developing countries where a lack of money and knowledge prevents people from getting the treatment needed to recover. In their infectious state, they infect millions of others every year, many of whom will die.

AIDS is likely to make the problem worse. "As HIV makes people more vulnerable to tuberculosis and tuberculosis goes on to kill people with HIV, these dual epidemics have together become the most serious public health threat of the decade," Peter Piot, executive director of the Joint United Nations Programme on HIV/AIDS, stated.

Loss of Productivity

TB periodically strikes the middle class in the United States. But in this country, it seems likely to remain a disease of the poor, the homeless, the addicted, and the chronically ill, groups seldom represented significantly in the workforce.

In other countries, however, TB is already infecting the workforce to such an extent that productivity is being impacted. India, which has one-third of the world's TB cases, loses more than $13 billion in productivity each year because of TB. Other countries experience appreciable losses as well. If the current epidemic goes unchecked, it is likely that productivity will be increasingly affected as more people fall ill and are incapacitated by the disease.

Loss of Talent in Health-Related Fields

Deadly drug-resistant strains of TB are having a serious emotional impact on people who work in medicine and other health-related careers where risk of infection is high. Many who regularly come in contact with tubercular patients are infected and are waiting to see if they will fall ill. A few have already died.

So great is the risk that some workers are rethinking their commitment to health care. "When I started in medicine the prospect of being exposed to TB was not a big deal since there were drugs to treat it, but now it's a life-threatening disease," says one doctor who is infected but not showing symptoms.

Experts worry that the risk of catching TB could have a serious impact on career plans for thousands of young

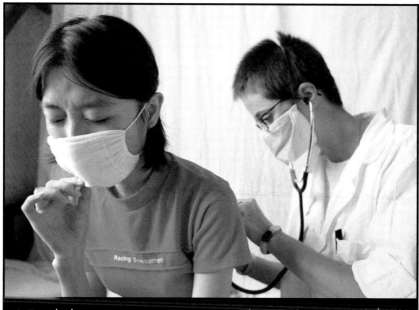

A French doctor examines a TB patient in China. Both patient and doctor wear masks to protect against the spread of TB within the hospital.

people who would otherwise be interested in going into medicine or working in health-related fields. At a time when the need for the finest minds in science is the greatest—particularly in tuberculosis research—many may choose less risky careers, making the task of solving the TB problem much more difficult.

Growing Health Costs

If TB continues its spread into suburban and small-town America, the cost of prevention and control, especially for communities with limited budgets, is likely to be staggering. Medicine and treatment for an ordinary case of TB cost about two thousand dollars, but treating resistant strains can run into the thousands for drugs alone. Medical care for resistant cases can total more than one-quarter of a million dollars per patient.

Poor countries already find themselves more financially restricted than small U.S. communities. Their poverty is deeper, and they have greater numbers of TB cases to deal with. Since untreated tuberculosis is a global problem, international organizations and economically stable nations such as the United States may find it in their own best interests to contribute generously to international TB control, especially to help economically impoverished countries that cannot find the funds for effective treatment. As the head of one antituberculosis project wrote, "To protect Americans against this deadly lung disease, the federal government must make an immediate commitment to controlling TB in the most severely affected nations of the world. Unless we provide appropriate therapy for those who are sick, we cannot continue to make headway against TB in the United States."

PERSONAL LIBERTY VERSUS PUBLIC HEALTH

As they face a variety of medical and social problems posed by the growing TB threat, legislators, health experts, and others in the United States grapple with legal controversies raised by detention programs designed to control the spread of multidrug-resistant tuberculosis. The controversy revolves around a patient's right to reject treatment as opposed to the government's right to isolate those who refuse to take their medicine. Should people who are sick be detained—in some cases, imprisoned—because they pose a threat to public health, or does such a position violate the principles of freedom for which the United States stands? Civil libertarians insist that detention of anyone who has not committed a crime is unjustifiable. Others believe that public health must come first and that it is time to revive that old institution, the sanitorium, in which patients can be quarantined while receiving treatment to recover from their disease.

The issue of detention is not a new one in the United States. In the early 1900s, many people, most of them poor, were taken from their families and forcibly held in state sanitoriums and hospitals until they recovered or died. Laws that allow health officials to confine tuberculosis victims remain on the books in at least forty states, holdovers from that earlier time. The AIDS epidemic of the 1980s reintroduced the issue of detention when fresh attempts were made to isolate those who were infected. Only concerted efforts by patients, doctors, and advocates established patients' rights and helped protect them from quarantine and possible discrimination.

Drug-resistant strains of tuberculosis make the present discussion of detention and quarantine reasonable, perhaps crucial. TB is more contagious than AIDS and almost as deadly. If those who are infectious refuse treatment, the consequences can be extremely serious. Yet civil libertarians fear that human-rights violations may result if thousands of individuals are incarcerated against their will. Richard Coker, in his 2000 book *From Chaos to Coercion: Detention and the Control of Tuberculosis*, criticizes the use of detention by many cities in the 1990s, noting that the poor and underprivileged were detained far more often than others. He argues that detention can be part of a just system of public-health care but that historically it has been over-used and that it has contributed to social problems even as it alleviates the public-health burden.

Despite the protests, many cities and states have elected to protect the public's health, even if that means temporarily depriving individuals of their freedom. "Nobody wants to create a gulag [prison] for the difficult patient," states Dr. David Rothman, a Columbia University physician who helped form guidelines for detention in New York City. "But when all else fails we need to face an unpleasant fact: When you balance the principles of liberty with a threat to the public health, liberty occasionally has to suffer."

Tuberculosis continues to test the intelligence and cre-ativity of the best minds in the world, but most are con-vinced that the disease can be eradicated if everyone makes a concerted effort to bring it under control. Despite apa-thy, ignorance, and debate, much is already being done by governments, hospitals, and private interests, especially in the United States. The headway they are making is explored in greater depth in the next chapter.

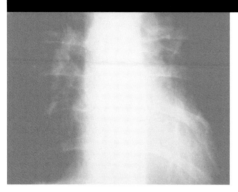

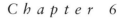

ACTION AND AWARENESS

In the 1950s, renowned TB expert René Dubos observed, "The problem of tuberculosis control is . . . dominated by economic considerations. What is the cost of the disease to the community? How much can society afford to devote to medical and public-health measures?" Those same considerations apply to the problem of TB control today. Many of the disease's victims are poor and unable to afford health care. Many of the countries that have serious outbreaks of TB are poor as well. A lack of attention and money has given the disease a head start that makes it difficult to combat and impossible to eliminate quickly.

Through a combination of action and awareness, the epidemic can be brought under control, however. In the United States, officials have set up effective guidelines for treatment, implemented them, and seen positive results— the incidence of new cases of tuberculosis in 2006 is almost half of what it was at its peak in 1992, and numbers of new cases continue to decline. Other nations are following the lead of the United States. From Washington, D.C., to Geneva, Switzerland, and from Moscow to Mexico, experts work to improve awareness of tuberculosis, to garner support for TB programs, and to find solutions to problems that hinder the containment of this global killer.

GOVERNMENT INVOLVEMENT

Throughout the world, health officials work to convince noncompliant governments of the wisdom and cost-effectiveness of funding and supporting TB programs before the number of cases balloons beyond control.

The cost of negligence was demonstrated in the United States in 1990. Prior to that time, the government believed TB to be at an all-time low in the nation and estimated that it would take only $36 million a year to wipe out the disease by the year 2010. Funds had not been set aside for the task, however, and after ignoring TB for decades, officials discovered to their dismay that the number of cases had risen dramatically and was continuing to do so. Eradication was no longer a near-term possibility, and projected costs of controlling the epidemic were stunning. New York City alone spent $700 million dollars between 1992 and 1996 on tuberculosis efforts.

However, other countries were not able to devote the same level of resources to tuberculosis. Russia in the 1990s experienced an epidemic similar to that of New York City's. TB infection and death rates doubled there between 1991 and 1997, earning the country one of the highest mortality rates in Europe. The government was unable to combat the problem effectively—the economy was severely strained after the fall of Communism in 1991, the standard of living had fallen greatly, and officials hesitated to adopt directly observed therapy programs. Thus, in 2005, more than 170,000 new cases of TB were registered. Many of these cases originated in prisons, where fully one-half of the country's 1 million inmates became infected with the bacteria and 10 percent exhibited active cases. Due to the crudeness of the facilities and lack of proper medical treatment, infection easily spread from prisoners to guards to medical staff. Latent infections that became active after prisoners were released allowed them to pass their infections—many of them deadly drug-resistant strains—to the general population.

The Russian government has been taking steps to halt the epidemic, but many obstacles remain. In recent years, the budget for tuberculosis has increased dramatically and

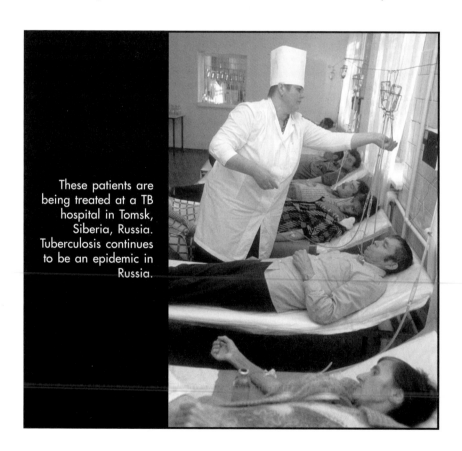

These patients are being treated at a TB hospital in Tomsk, Siberia, Russia. Tuberculosis continues to be an epidemic in Russia.

the rate of new infections is gradually slowing, but there is still much work to be done.

EFFORTS OF WORLD HEALTH AGENCIES

A vast number of organizations are working to improve public health and encourage awareness of and action against the problem of tuberculosis worldwide. Two of the most effective and prestigious are the World Health Organization, headquartered in Geneva, Switzerland, and the Centers for Disease Control and Prevention, located in Atlanta, Georgia.

Part of the United Nations, the World Health Organization was established in 1948. Designed to be the world authority on all international health issues, its goals are to promote technical cooperation for health among nations, carry out programs to control and eradicate disease, and strive to improve the quality of human life. In 2007 the organization included 193 member countries.

One of the projects sponsored by the World Health Organization is World TB Day, established in 1982 on the one-hundredth anniversary of Robert Koch's announcement of his discovery of the tuberculosis bacterium. An international health event, World TB Day is not a celebration but a reminder that one of the worst public-health threats of all time is still at work and that it is time to mobilize public support to finally eradicate it.

In 1995 WHO declared tuberculosis a global emergency, the first time the organization had ever taken such a position. According to WHO, one person becomes infected with TB every second and an estimated one-third of the world's population is infected with TB. In the twenty-first century, the main objective of the WHO tuberculosis program is to encourage the wider implementation of DOTS programs. More than 183 countries have already adopted DOTS strategies for controlling and eliminating TB. This number includes 22 "high-burden" countries, including Brazil, Nigeria, and Thailand, which together account for 80 percent of the world's TB cases. However, in some countries, DOTS is still only available in limited areas. WHO also concentrates on retraining those who staff TB programs worldwide, since many are ignorant of and resistant to changes in health policies.

As its global objective, WHO called for detection of 70 percent of all new cases and curing of 85 percent of those cases worldwide by the year 2005. While those goals were not met, WHO still achieved remarkable success in reducing rates of TB.

In 2006 the World Health Organization began a new ten-year strategy to stop the global tuberculosis epidemic. The Global Plan to Stop TB aims to eliminate TB as a public-health problem by not only expanding DOTS across the world but also by funding research into new ways to combat TB and by strengthening health-care systems across the world. The goal is to eliminate TB as a public-health crisis by reducing the number of cases to only one person per one million people by the year 2050.

Another highly regarded health organization, the Centers for Disease Control and Prevention, is an arm of the U.S. Public Health Service. Established as the Communicable Disease Center in 1946, the agency became the Centers for Disease Control in 1970. The words *and Prevention* were added in 1992.

The CDC conducts research into the origin and occurrence of various diseases throughout the world and develops methods to control and eradicate them. Involved with tuberculosis for decades, the agency has established three tuberculosis research centers in the United States and collaborates with numerous health agencies and health departments to improve the effectiveness of tuberculosis control programs. The CDC laboratories in Atlanta, Georgia, are some of the nation's

The headquarters of the Centers for Disease Control and Prevention is in Atlanta, Georgia.

few containment facilities—equipped with specialized protective equipment—where researchers can work with dangerous drug-resistant strains of TB in safety.

The CDC supports an action plan against tuberculosis that includes using existing prevention and control methods more effectively, developing new methods and materials to be used in diagnosis, treatment, and prevention and speeding up the transfer of such newly developed technologies to clinics and public-health facilities throughout the world.

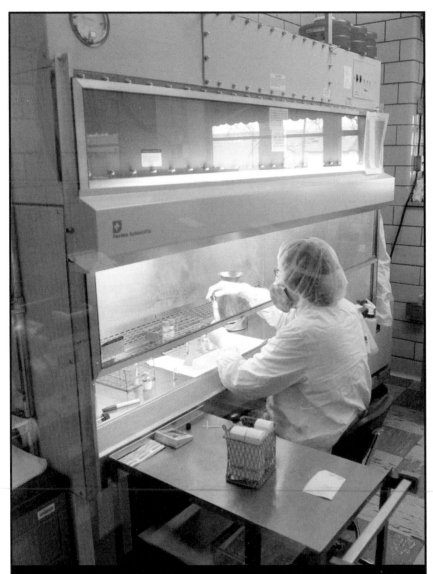

A microbiologist tests possible tuberculosis specimens under a ventilation hood at the West Virginia Office of Laboratory Services (OLS) in South Charleston, West Virginia. The OLS is one of the regional levels of protection created by the CDC to help guard public health.

In 1998 the CDC presented a plan for federal, state, and local TB control programs to address TB among foreign-born populations in the United States. Recommendations include identifying individuals who are infected or who are at high risk, developing creative means of overcoming obstacles to TB diagnosis and care, and maximizing activities to ensure completion of treatment. Presently, immigrants with active TB are allowed to enter the United States provided that they immediately seek treatment. Many do not seek such treatment, however, and overburdened health departments and clinics lack resources necessary for locating them and then ensuring that they get complete, effective care.

Beginning in 1999, the CDC began working with the U.S. Agency for International Development (USAID) to provide financial and technical assistance to tuberculosis programs across the world. Since 1998 more than $400 million has gone to high-risk countries such as Russia, South Africa, and the Philippines.

PRIVATE PHILANTHROPY

As TB continues to threaten the world, a number of charities and wealthy individuals have made large donations toward programs aimed at ending the disease. These donors have not only given substantial monetary support to such programs, but they have made the global tuberculosis epidemic more visible, drawing attention to a previously under-rated problem.

The Global Fund to Fight AIDS, Tuberculosis, and Malaria was founded in 2002. Although it has ties to the World Health Organization, it is a separate entity. Unlike WHO, the Global Fund does not directly implement programs. Rather, it finances and monitors programs around the world, leaving the actual fight against disease to local experts. For example, the Global Fund provided a grant to Sierra Leone in Africa to help rebuild 70 percent of that nation's DOTS treatment centers, which were destroyed in its civil war.

To date, the Global Fund has committed more than $7 billion, approximately 17 percent of which is spent on TB programs. While much of the funding comes from governments, the Global Fund has also received substantial donations from private individuals. In August 2006, for example, the Bill and Melinda Gates Foundation announced that it would give more than $500 million over the following five years. The Gates Foundation and others have contributed enormously to the fight against tuberculosis in the twenty-first century.

Bill *(center)* and Melinda *(right)* Gates listen to a TB patient describe how he has lived with and been treated for his illness in South Africa. The Bill and Melinda Gates Foundation has donated more than half a billion dollars to the global fight against TB, AIDS, and malaria.

NATIONAL, REGIONAL, AND LOCAL EFFORTS

On national, regional, and local levels, health departments and other health agencies continue to do their part to control TB by educating the public about the threat of infection, by utilizing the most effective combinations of therapies, by setting up better health-care systems to prevent infection, and by enlisting more and better trained staff to investigate, monitor, and ensure recovery of those who are ill.

Existing efforts need to be intensified and expanded, however. Incentive systems like those established in cities such as Denver, Colorado, yield excellent results, but most of these efforts remain local and rely on broad-minded authorities and healthy city budgets to survive. DOTS programs are relatively inexpensive to run, extremely effective, and can save cities millions of dollars in health costs, but they still reach only a small percentage of TB cases throughout the world. The work, cost, and commitment involved in setting up DOTS programs in every region of the world is daunting but necessary unless other effective approaches can be found.

In addition to expanding and improving health services, health officials must also concentrate on creating nonthreatening environments for those who are at high risk but who habitually shun health care. For instance, U.S. policies that aim to restrict health-care services to undocumented people have the potential of making the TB problem worse, since those who are ill risk deportation if they seek treatment. Even legal immigrants who fled persecution in other countries are likely to be suspicious and inclined to avoid doctors and clinics, which they see as being linked to authority.

THE ROLE OF CLINICS AND HOSPITALS

Clinics and hospitals must continue to improve safety conditions in their facilities, by installing bacteria-killing ultraviolet lights in all offices and examination rooms and by educating patients to cover their mouths and noses when they cough and sneeze. Money needs to be set aside for proper ventilation systems that push contaminated air outside rather than recirculating it throughout buildings. The same is true for isolation rooms that maintain negative pressure so that contaminated air does not flow out into corridors when doors are opened.

Agreement needs to be reached regarding safety precautions that medical personnel should take as they work with TB infected patients. Some follow stringent guidelines that require them to wear heavy rubber masks connected to a motorized air pump on a belt when they examine patients. Others consider such measures impractical and prefer to make do with a simple cloth or paper mask. Many doctors adopt the latter practice, convinced that trust and rapport is damaged if they cannot speak to their clients when they treat them. Explains Dr. Lee Reichman, "We have to build relations with sick patients, and if doctors have to get into spacesuits and wear gas masks, patients aren't going to take their pills. It's probably much more important to teach TB patents to cover their mouths when they cough."

Hospitals should also aim to employ the most up-to-date and effective treatment regimens they can afford. The National Jewish Medical and Research Center in Denver is one example of what a fine TB facility can do, given enough money, creativity, and dedication. Services at National Jewish include inpatient and outpatient clinics, rehabilitation facilities, and psychosocial support for long-term treatment. Well-equipped, up-to-date laboratories allow workers to identify unknown strains of *M. tuberculosis*, test for resistance to all drugs, and quickly determine the exact level of medication needed to suppress bacterial growth, thus maximizing benefits to each patient while minimizing side effects. A consultation phone line allows physicians outside the hospital and around the world to

National Jewish Medical and Research Center in Denver, Colorado, is one of the top hospitals in the United States for the treatment of TB. The hospital specializes in respiratory disorders of all types.

get advice regarding effective drug therapy, length of therapy, appropriate isolation procedures, the need for surgical intervention, and other issues. Training sessions for doctors, nurses, and other health professionals who deal with TB are offered three times a year. "This course [is] a boot camp to recruit soldiers for a war," states Dr. Michael Iseman, a top TB specialist at the center.

Using a combination of drugs and radical surgery, Iseman and other top-notch physicians and surgeons who work at National Jewish are able to effect a 90 percent cure rate among their TB clientele, many of whom have multidrug-resistant tuberculosis and have been pronounced incurable by other physicians and specialists.

RESPONSIBILITY OF SCHOOLS

School administrators need to be aware that TB is a very real danger to students, especially if districts serve poor, immigrant, and minority families who are at higher risk. Officials should be aware of the risk factors that prevail in their particular region and should have a good school health program in place in order to deal promptly and effectively with infection should TB cases arise. "Schools need to take TB very seriously," says one school principal. To those who like to think that TB won't hit their school, he says, "When you're in a public place, there is always a risk."

SOLUTIONS IN CORRECTIONAL FACILITIES

Prisons, too, need to focus on making their environs safer. Many correctional facilities in the United States are already doing so. In New York City, where no jail had separately ventilated cells in 1992 and where almost one in five prisoners tested positive for TB at that time, improvements have been dramatic in some cases. Rikers Island, one of the biggest prisons in New York State, has spent millions to create a computerized tracing system for prisoners with TB, to screen most inmates with a chest X-ray at the time of their arrest, and to build properly ventilated isolation cells that cost almost half a million dollars each. Rikers Island's new system is considered a model in the prison world.

Smaller jails may not have the space and funds to do as much, but those who run them are becoming more aware of the risks of TB and doing what they can to create safer conditions for inmates. Since there are no precise specifications to guide planners as they upgrade old buildings to meet new safety recommendations, however, money is often wasted on efforts that do not work—ventilation systems so noisy that inmates cannot sleep and ultraviolet lights so bright that they cause headache and eyestrain. Guidelines need to be established to help cash-strapped establishments effectively improve their facilities.

PERSONAL EFFORTS

While governments and health agencies do their part to fight TB, ordinary individuals need to be aware of what they can do to lower their risk of becoming infected and ill. The danger is not so great as to justify extreme measures—in most cases, simple, straightforward precautions are enough. People are encouraged to maintain healthy, active lifestyles and to avoid possible factors that put them at risk for infection (drug abuse and alcoholism, for example). Good health generally promotes high resistance, enabling the body's defenses to fight off TB infection. "We're glad we were in good shape physically," David says. "I like to think that Denise stayed healthy, and the baby and I got well fast, because we take care of ourselves. I can only imagine how hard it is to cope with TB when you're old or sick with AIDS."

Panic is unwarranted, but no one should assume that he or she is exempt from becoming infected with tuberculosis. In particular, one should be aware of the risks if one is poor, in poor health, elderly, or a health-care worker. If you believe you may have been exposed to TB, get a skin test and preventive treatment if necessary. If you experience symptoms of tuberculosis, go to your doctor and follow the prescribed regimen of antibiotics until you are well.

OTHER EFFORTS

As situations arise, other agencies need to be alert to the need for guidelines and restrictions that can help protect the public from tuberculosis. Such has been the case with airlines carrying passengers who may have active TB on extended flights. Studies show that one individual with active disease can infect four or five others during flights of over eight hours' duration. With more than one billion passengers traveling by air annually, the possibility of travelers becoming infected is very real. "As a pilot up in the cockpit, I'm somewhat isolated," says Jodi's father, "but flight attendants and passengers are right out there, exposed to anything that comes along. On crowded flights—well, you just have to hope your resistance is high and no one is sick with anything serious."

To head off potential problems, the Centers for Disease Control and Prevention worked with airline companies, health authorities, doctors, and airline passengers to come up with guidelines, which essentially recommend that those with infectious TB refrain from traveling by air until they are not contagious. If it is discovered that someone with infectious TB has been on a flight of more than eight hours, passengers and crew in the same section of the plane should be promptly informed of their exposure and instructed to see their doctor for screening and preventive treatment. The case in 2007 in which Andrew Speaker traveled overseas and back despite having drug-resistant tuberculosis (discussed in chapter 2) is a prime example of the need for greater security.

A TENACIOUS FOE

Experts are no longer as optimistic as they once were about eliminating the threat of tuberculosis in the near future. They understand that it is a difficult, tenacious, changeable, and destructive adversary, particularly in conditions of poverty, ill health, and ignorance. Although *M. tuberculosis* is likely to be defeated by modern medicine sometime in the future, the battle promises to be long and arduous. One of the chief difficulties that experts face is a general lack of interest in a disease that is neither "sexy" nor sensational. However, this is slowly changing, as organizations such as the Global Fund and the Bill and

Melinda Gates Foundation bring publicity to the fight against tuberculosis. "TB science has advanced significantly over the past five years," says Dr. Tachi Yamada, president of the Gates Foundation's Global Health Program. "By bringing together a wide range of partners, including scientists from countries heavily affected by TB, we hope to help translate promising ideas into tools that can save millions of lives."

The outlook for the future is brighter than many once thought due to the skill and ingenuity of fine minds around the world. Further progress that is being made against tuberculosis both in research and in people's everyday lives will be discussed in greater depth in chapter 7.

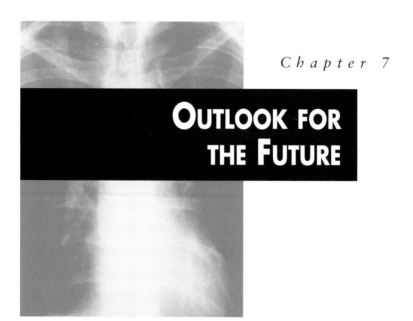

OUTLOOK FOR THE FUTURE

Tuberculosis presents a formidable challenge to health workers. They need more reliable vaccines, rapid and cost-effective diagnostic techniques, and new drugs to better combat the epidemic in the future. Because interest had been focused on other medical problems such as AIDS and cancer, few researchers had been working to make such breakthroughs. "This old disease is so poorly understood at a cellular level," says Dr. Charles Nolan, a TB expert from Seattle. "As a friend of mine said, in this era of molecular biology, we're still diagnosing TB by looking at a bump on the forearm." He points out that the skin test was developed decades ago and that most anti-TB drugs were discovered or invented during or before the 1970s.

A significant number of health and research centers are now trying to correct such biomedical shortcomings. They are working hard not just to control and prevent tuberculosis but to better understand it, particularly on a molecular level. In the future, they hope to learn more about how *M. tuberculosis* interacts with human cells, how it generates granulomas, how and why the human immune system sometimes beats TB back and sometimes succumbs to it, and what factors effect latency and reactivation.

A complete understanding of tuberculosis will take time, but many tantalizing facts are being uncovered and some long-standing questions seem likely to be answered in the near future.

How does TB become resistant to drugs?

Researchers discovered in 1992 that the loss of a specific gene during the mutation process makes *M. tuberculosis* resistant to treatment with isoniazid. Reinserting the missing gene causes the bacterium to again become susceptible to this drug. Researchers also identified the site on *M. tuberculosis* that is attacked by isoniazid, paving the way for the design of drugs that will specifically target that site. Understanding at the molecular level how tuberculosis develops resistance to one drug may help scientists conquer drug resistance in total someday in the future.

Further progress in understanding the molecular structure and function of *M. tuberculosis* will take place now that researchers at the Pasteur Institute in Paris and the Sanger Centre in Great Britain have succeeded in decoding the enormous, complex genetic code of the bacterium—in effect, identifying every gene in its makeup. The project is a landmark in research. Only a dozen such bacterial genomes (genetic identities) have been unraveled since 1995, and only one was larger than *M. tuberculosis*.

Determining the function of each of the bacterium's four thousand genes will take time, but knowing the DNA sequence will help experts better understand the microbe and will open up vast new possibilities for TB research. For instance, investigators are already looking at one specific gene that may account for *M. tuberculosis*'s ability to become dormant for years in the lung before developing into active disease.

How can doctors speed diagnoses and save lives?

A relatively new procedure, DNA fingerprinting, also called DNA typing, has the potential to be a valuable tool in the diagnosis, analysis, and identification of tuberculosis. The technique involves the comparison of fragments of genetic material found within all living things. Because each strain of M. *tuberculosis* has its own distinct DNA fingerprint, lab workers can use those fingerprints to classify strains, identify clusters of individuals who have been infected from a common source, and ensure that proper and effective antibiotics are prescribed to bring about a more rapid cure.

This DNA fingerprinting device can be used to quickly identify diseases. TB researchers are hopeful DNA fingerprinting will help identify particularly dangerous forms of TB before they become more drug resistant.

Researchers have come up with another genetic test whereby the presence of tuberculosis bacteria can be determined by examination of a patient's sputum. The process does not identify whether the strain is drug resistant, but it is as quick as a chest X-ray, and does not pose a risk for cancer.

An experimental process that promises to help doctors quickly select drugs to which a particular TB strain is susceptible involves inserting the gene that makes fireflies glow into a virus that infects M. tuberculosis. Research workers treat M. tuberculosis with the drug they wish to test and then expose it to the altered virus. If the M. tuberculosis bacteria remain alive (showing that they are resistant to the drug), they give off a dim yellowish-green light as the virus successfully infects them. If the M. tuberculosis bacteria die (showing that they are susceptible to the drug), no light appears because the virus cannot infect them.

A procedure that uses fluorescent "molecular beacons"—molecules of nucleic acids that make up DNA—to identify multidrug-resistant strains of tuberculosis may also help ensure that infected people get treatment as quickly as possible. The procedure, which highlights mutated portions of the M. tuberculosis bacteria, signifying drug resistance, takes three hours instead of several weeks to carry out and has proven highly accurate in early trials.

What more can be done to ensure that patients take medications correctly?

Researchers are working to come up with new strategies to make it easier for TB patients to take their medication for the full course of treatment. Some scientists believe that a promising alternative to pills might be an implant—a tiny, flexible tube filled with medication placed under the skin—that could release drugs into the body over a period of months with no effort on the part of the patient. An implant would ensure that patients received medication on time and would reduce the burden on field-workers involved in DOTS programs.

While pills remain the standard for treatment, those like Rifater and Rifapentine allow patients to take fewer doses, thus relieving them of the burden of a strict daily regimen for at least some medications. Researchers are trying to develop other drugs that will be effective, less likely to induce drug resistance, and entail fewer side effects. "Tuberculosis cannot be fully controlled with existing medications," says Anthony S. Fauci of the National Institutes of Allergy and Infectious Diseases (NIAID). "We desperately need new drugs to combat this worldwide public health problem."

Are there ways to boost a person's resistance to tuberculosis?

A study performed at the University of Colorado suggests that vitamin D, produced in humans during exposure to sunlight, may be important in boosting the body's resistance to tuberculosis. Researchers found that the vitamin, converted to a different form by the liver, helped macrophages slow or stop the replication of M. *tuberculosis*. The findings support age-old beliefs that exposure to sunlight helps cure the disease.

If there is a correlation between vitamin D and resistance, the possibility exists that the incidence of tuberculosis in developing countries could be decreased by improving diets or supplementing them with vitamin D. The vitamin is already routinely added to milk in the United States.

Will there be new treatments for TB in the future?

Undoubtedly, researchers in the future will identify methods besides antibiotics and surgery to treat tuberculosis. One possible therapy could make use of a chemical, osteopontin, which scientists discovered in 1997. Produced by the body when it is infected with TB, osteopontin appears to act as a signal for defense cells to form granulomas. Researchers hope to utilize their new knowledge of the chemical to boost the body's ability to fight tuberculosis even in patients who show low resistance to the disease.

Will there be a new vaccine for tuberculosis soon?

A variety of projects designed to create a better tuberculosis vaccine are under way across the world, and a significant portion of global funding goes toward programs that are working to develop new vaccines. Some aim to improve the BCG vaccine. Researchers at two institutes are creating newly engineered forms of BCG that are already more effective in producing an immune response in mice. Other scientists seek to develop an entirely new product. The most welcome vaccine would be one that

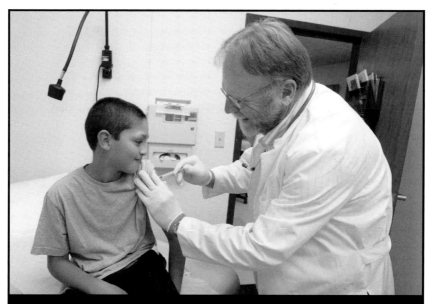

A health-care worker administers a vaccine to a boy in San Jose, California. Many school districts, such as the one in San Jose, require a number of vaccines and a TB test before children can enter school. Researchers continue to search for an effective and safe TB vaccine to add to those other vaccines already in use.

prevents disease rather than infection, since it could be used for those who are already infected and would effectively prevent the onset of new cases. Such a product would need to be relatively free of side effects and safe to use on HIV-infected individuals and others with weakened immune systems. One scientist is even working on a vaccine that can be inhaled rather than injected and that would thus be far easier to transport and administer.

Efforts to develop a vaccine appear promising, and experts at the CDC believe that several possibilities will be ready for human testing in the next few years. "If we can put a man on the moon within a decade . . . we can come up with a new TB vaccine and eliminate TB in the United States," says Dr. Richard O'Brien of the CDC.

SUCCESS STORIES

While researchers concentrate on biomedical aspects of tuberculosis, they never forget the personal consequences of having the disease—the fear, pain, and suffering that people like David, Randall, Sonia, and Jodi experience as they struggle to get well and get on with their lives. Fortunately, despite unanswered questions in the laboratory, the clinical outlook for people with tuberculosis is positive. Those individuals who conscientiously follow their doctors' instructions are able to recover. Success stories far outnumber failures in the battle to conquer the disease.

David—"There Are Scars"

The source of the tuberculosis in David's family is likely to remain unknown, since investigators have been unable to trace a case of active disease to anyone outside the family. Denise remains symptom free as do members of David's law firm, although three of them tested positive for TB and were treated with isoniazid to prevent illness.

David and Denise worried throughout the wait for test results but were finally assured that their strain of TB was not a drug-resistant variety. "We have family members who were sure we were going to die," Denise said. "It was a horrible, scary time." Thanks to proper antibiotic treatment and Denise's efforts to ensure they complied with their doctor's instructions, David and Mica's symptoms disappeared after two months. Today both are again in good health and show no signs of the ordeal they have undergone. "We feel lucky compared to some. We were able to get back to normal so quickly," David says. "On the other hand, there are scars. We've lost some friends. We don't go into the city unless we have to. And when somebody coughs at the grocery store, my heart beats faster. I don't take our health for granted anymore. I don't think I ever will."

Randall—An Uncertain End

Randall's wife and one of his children tested positive for tuberculosis infection. Doctors prescribed medication other than isoniazid as a preventive, since Randall's strain was resistant to that antibiotic.

Randall remained in Miami for a time and then left town, resurfacing in New York City. On a visit to a clinic there, health officials learned of his record of noncompliance with treatment and hospitalized him, placing him on an intense regimen of medications for several weeks until he was no longer infectious. "I can't hang around here too long," he told a health-care worker who was assigned to supervise his pill taking after his release. "I want to be near my kids."

Sonia—Cautiously Hopeful

Sonia spent almost a year at National Jewish Medical and Research Center, undergoing treatment that doctors hoped would save her life. "I was very sick and my family was far away. The doctors and nurses were the best—very professional, very hopeful. But no one could take away the fear and the loneliness."

To treat Sonia's highly resistant strain of bacteria, doctors prescribed a strict course of drugs, some of which killed germs, others that suppressed the many side effects Sonia suffered. They also resorted to pneumothorax to reduce oxygen to infected tissues and slow the progress of the disease.

After months of careful treatment, the day came when Sonia's sputum tests were germfree. Her troubles were not over yet, however. Despite progress, her left lung had been irreparably damaged by the disease and had to be surgically removed. Once she recovered from surgery, she was allowed to return home. "I still take my medicines regularly and will have to for some time," Sonia explains. "But I'm getting along well. I can see my family and friends again. Someday I hope to go back to work and get on with my life."

Jodi—Breathing Easier

The source of Jodi's illness was finally traced to one of the students in her class, a teen who had immigrated to the United States with his family from Southeast Asia several years before. "He may have been infected before coming to the United States," says one local health official. "There's a lot of TB in his homeland of Vietnam. He did all the right things when he began feeling sick—went to the doctor, stayed home from school a few days. It's just that no one noticed that his symptoms were classic TB. No one put two and two together and said. 'Hey, he's had a bad cough for a month and he's coughing up lots of phlegm. It sounds like tuberculosis.'"

Jodi took antibiotics regularly and, after several weeks, was judged noninfectious and was able to return to school. She continued to take medication for six months, and her mother made sure she took every pill on schedule. Because Jodi responded well to treatment, doctors were reassured that her strain was not drug resistant.

"It seems like it's a happy ending, so we can all breathe easier," Jodi's father says. "This whole episode has been a real lesson for us, though. No one should be unconcerned about TB. It's out there. It's serious. But we're proof that it can be controlled. Maybe one day it'll be gone for good. Just another long-gone killer that we read about in the pages of history. I look forward to that day."

GLOSSARY

acute: having a rapid onset and following a short but severe course

AIDS (acquired immunodeficiency syndrome): a severe disorder of the immune system caused by a virus. AIDS results in increased susceptibility to opportunistic infections and to certain cancers.

alveolus: one of many tiny air sacs deep in the lungs, where the exchange of oxygen and carbon dioxide takes place

antibiotic: a substance such as penicillin or streptomycin that destroys or inhibits the growth of microorganisms and is used to treat infectious diseases

bacillus: a rod-shaped bacterium

Bacillus Calmette-Guerin (BCG) vaccine: a preparation designed to provide protection against TB, named after French scientists Calmette and Guerin

bacterium: any of a number of single-cell microorganisms that exist in various shapes and are associated with processes of decay, fermentation, and the cause of disease in plants and animals

biomedicine: the study of medicine as it relates to biological systems

bronchoscope: a medical device that, when inserted down

the trachea and into the bronchial tubes, enables a physician to examine the bronchial surface

caseous: soft, cheeselike

cavity: an area of diseased tissue in the lung where TB bacteria have caused destruction of tissue. Patients with cavities in their lungs are more likely to cough up bacteria and to be infectious.

chemotherapy: treatment of disease using specific chemical agents or drugs

chronic: of long duration; continuing or lingering

consumption: an early term for pulmonary tuberculosis

contact: a person who has spent time with someone who has infectious TB

culture: microorganisms grown in a specially prepared nutrient medium

directly observed therapy, short-course (DOTS): a method of helping TB patients take their medications properly. Using DOTS, a health-care worker meets with a patient every day or several times a week at a prearranged spot, such as a clinic, a patient's home or work, or other convenient place. During the meeting, the worker observes and verifies that the patient has taken the required medication.

DNA (deoxyribonucleic acid): genetic material found in all cellular organisms and most viruses

epidemiology: the branch of medicine that studies the causes, distribution, and control of disease in populations

extrapulmonary TB: TB disease in any part of the body other than the lungs

genome: the complete collection of an organism's genetic material

hemoptysis: the coughing or spitting up of blood from the respiratory tract

hemorrhage: copious or excessive bleeding

HIV infection: infection with the human immunodeficiency virus that causes AIDS

Hodgkin's disease: cancer of the lymphatic system, which is important in removing and destroying toxic substances and in resisting the spread of disease

immune system: system of organs, tissues, cells, and cell products such as antibodies that fight potentially harmful organisms or substances in the body

immunology: the branch of medicine dealing with the immune system

isoniazid: an antibiotic used to prevent TB disease in people infected with the bacteria. Isoniazid is also used to treat TB disease.

lymph nodes: round or oval bodies, part of the lymph system, that help remove bacteria and foreign particles from the body

macrophage: a large cell that engulfs and absorbs foreign bodies in the blood stream and tissues

Mantoux skin test: a test used to detect TB infection. A skin test entails injecting a small amount of liquid called tuberculin under the skin in the lower part of the arm and then waiting to see if the body reacts to it.

miliary TB: an acute form of TB disease, caused by the spread of bacteria throughout the body. The disease is characterized by small tubercles in various body organs.

multidrug-resistant tuberculosis (MDR-TB): TB disease caused by bacteria that are resistant to more than one anti-tubercular drug

negative: referring to a test result for TB. A negative TB skin test reaction means that a person is probably not infected with TB

opportunistic infections: infections by organisms that do not normally cause disease except in people whose immune systems have been weakened

pneumonectomy: surgical removal of all or part of a lung

pneumothorax: a procedure used to treat tuberculosis whereby air is pumped into the abdominal or chest cavity to compress the lungs and reduce oxygen in an infected area

positive: referring to a test result for TB. A positive TB skin test reaction means that a person has been infected with TB

Pott's disease: partial destruction of the vertebrae, usually caused by tuberculosis, and often producing curvature of the spine

Pulmonary TB: tuberculosis occurring in the lungs

sanitorium: an institution for the treatment and supervision of patients with a chronic disease such as tuberculosis

scrofula: a form of tuberculosis affecting the lymph nodes, particularly those of the neck

silocosis: a lung disease affecting individuals employed in mining, stonecutting, and similar industries

sputum: mucus and other material coughed up from the respiratory tract

TB disease: an illness caused by TB bacteria multiplying and invading different parts of the body. A person with TB disease will have symptoms such as coughing, night sweats, fever, and weight loss.

TB infection: a condition in which TB bacteria are alive but inactive in the human body. Individuals with TB infection have no symptoms and are not infectious but usually have a positive skin test reaction.

TB meningitis: tuberculosis disease of the brain and spinal chord, characterized by high fever, intense headache, nausea, stiff neck, and coma

uberculin: a liquid derived from tubercle bacilli and used in tests for tuberculosis

vaccine: a preparation—commonly a treated sample of microorganisms—that is injected into a person to produce increased immunity to a particular disease

RESOURCES

An extensive list of national and international organizations that provide information about tuberculosis can be accessed on the Internet under the key word "Tuberculosis." Or you can call or write:

American Lung Association (ALA)
61 Broadway
New York, NY 10006
1 (800) LUNG-USA (800-586-4872)
http://www.lungusa.org
The American Lung Association has been fighting lung disease through education, community service, advocacy, and research since 1904. It funds more than two hundred research grants, enabling medical scientists to seek the causes of lung disease and develop more effective treatment and cures. The organization publishes a wide variety of materials on topics relating to lung health, including asthma, tobacco use, and tuberculosis.

The Bill and Melinda Gates Foundation
P.O. Box 23350
Seattle, WA 98102
(206) 709-3100
http://www.gatesfoundation.org/
The Gates Foundation is the largest private philanthropic organization in the world, with an endowment of $33 billion. It funds a variety of programs across the world, including agricultural development in impoverished areas, improvements to libraries in the United States, and college scholarships for minority students. As of 2007, the foundation has spent or committed a total of $740 million to battle tuberculosis.

Centers for Disease Control and Prevention (CDC)
Division of Tuberculosis Elimination
1600 Clifton Road
Atlanta, GA 30333
1 (800) 311-3435
http://www.cdc.gov
The CDC conducts research into the origin and occurrence of various diseases throughout the world and develops methods to control and eradicate them. Involved in tuberculosis programs for decades, the agency

collaborates with numerous health agencies and health departments to improve the effectiveness of tuberculosis control and prevention. Fact sheets about tuberculosis are available on the Internet and by mail.

The Global Fund to Fight AIDS, Tuberculosis, and Malaria
Geneva Secretariat
Chemin de Blandonnet 8
1214 Vernier
Geneva, Switzerland
41 22 791 17 00
http://www.theglobalfund.org
The Global Fund was established in 2002 specifically as a way to increase the funding of global efforts to combat AIDS, tuberculosis, and malaria. The fund provides resources to programs across the world and will accept donations of any size.

International Union Against Tuberculosis and Lung Disease (IUATLD)
68 Boulevard Saint-Michel, F-75006
Paris, France
33 1 44 32 03 60
http://www.iuatld.org
Founded in Paris in 1920, the IUATLD is a nonprofit organization dedicated to the prevention and control of tuberculosis and lung disease, to providing information on the hazards of smoking, and to the promotion of overall community health. It advances its goals through conferences, classes, and publications that include a newsletter, health guides, and its official periodical the *International Journal of Tuberculosis and Lung Disease*. The IUATLD works closely with the World Health Organization.

National Institutes of Allergy and Infectious Diseases (NIAID)
NIAID Office of Communications and Public Liaison
6610 Rockledge Drive
MSC 6612
Bethesda, MD 20892-6612
(301) 496-5717
http://www3.niaid.nih.gov
An arm of the National Institutes of Health, NIAID supports and conducts biomedical research into the causes and prevention of tuberculosis, including basic research into the life processes of *M. tuberculosis*, development of new drugs and new methods to deliver standard drugs, vaccine development, training of TB researchers, and education of health-care workers and the public.

National Jewish Medical and Research Center
1400 Jackson Street
Denver, CO 80206
(303) 388-4461 or 1 (800) 222-LUNG (5864)
http://www.njc.org
Founded by the Jewish community in 1899 to care for poverty-stricken people with tuberculosis, National Jewish has become a global leader in the fight against lung, allergic, and immune diseases. A nonprofit institution, it is staffed by some of the best physicians in the United States, is renowned for its innovative cures, and has been ranked one of the top ten independent biomedical research centers in the world.

World Health Organization (WHO)
The Global Plan to Stop TB
Avenue Appia 20, CH-1211
Geneva 27, Switzerland
41 22 791 2630
http://www.who.int
A branch of the United Nations, the World Health Organization was established in 1948. Designed to be the world authority on all international health issues, it promotes cooperation among nations regarding public-health issues, implements programs to control and eradicate disease, and strives to improve the quality of human life. The Stop TB program led by the WHO is a multinational program dedicated to eradicating TB as a public-health issue by the year 2050.

FURTHER READING AND WEBSITES

FOR YOUNG READERS

Allman, Toney. *Tuberculosis.* Detroit: Lucent Books, 2006.
Ramen, Fred. *Tuberculosis.* New York: Rosen Publishing, 2001.
Silverstein, Alan, Virginia B. Silverstein, and Laura Silverstein Nunn.
  The Tuberculosis Update. Berkeley Heights, NJ: Enslow Publishers,
  2006.

FOR PARENTS AND TEACHERS

Coker, Richard J. *From Chaos to Coercion: Detention and the Control
  of Tuberculosis.* New York: St. Martin's Press, 2000.
Daniel, Thomas M. *Captain of Death: The Story of Tuberculosis.*
  Rochester, NY: University of Rochester Press, 1997.
Dubos, Rene, and Jean Dubos. *The White Plague.* Piscataway, NJ: Rut-
  gers University Press, 1987.
Gandy, Matthew, and Alimuddin Zumla. *The Return of the White
  Plague: Global Poverty and the 'New' Tuberculosis.* London: Verso,
  2003.
Ott, Katherine. *Fevered Lives: Tuberculosis in American Culture Since
  1870.* Cambridge, MA: Harvard University Press, 1999.
Reichman, Lee, and Janice Hopkins Tanne. *Timebomb: The Global
  Epidemic of Multi-Drug Resistant Tuberculosis.* New York:
  McGraw-Hill, 2003.

WEBSITES

Online Tuberculosis Information System (OTIS) Data
http://wonder.cdc.gov/tb.html
The Centers for Disease Control and Prevention's Online Tuberculosis
Information System lets users view tuberculosis statistics in the United
States from 1993 onward. These statistics can be broken down by year,
location, or a number of other criteria, including foreign- or U.S.-born,
HIV-positive or negative, or whether the tuberculosis is drug resistant
or not.

Stop TB Partnership
http://www.stoptb.org/
The Stop TB Partnership's website is constantly updated with news about antituberculosis efforts around the world.

Tuberculosis
http://www.mayoclinic.com/health/tuberculosis/DS00372
The Mayo Clinic site on tuberculosis is an excellent resource for basic information on tuberculosis symptoms and treatments.

For more information on the current tuberculosis epidemic and steps that are being taken to control it, search the Internet under the topic "Tuberculosis."

INDEX

acid-fast bacteria, 47
active disease, 49–50
African Americans, 19–20, 37–38
AIDS (acquired immunodeficiency syndrome), 7, 12, 28, 35–36, 53–54, 71–72
air travel, 42, 76–77, 101–102
alveoli, 48
anthrax, 22, 23
antibiotic therapy, 26, 61–62, 67
antibodies, 62–63
Asians, 38

Bacillus Calmette-Guerin (BCG) vaccine, 60–61, 108
Bill and Melinda Gates Foundation, 42, 96, 102–103
Bloom, Barry R., 28, 61
bones and joints, 52
Brehmer, Hermann, 24
bronchioles, 48
bronchoscopy, 40
Brontë, Charlotte, 17
Brontë, Emily, 17
bubonic plague, 13
Budd, William, 22
Byron, Lord, 18

Calmette, Albert, 60
caseous material, 48–49, 51
cavities, 38, 50
Centers for Disease Control and Prevention (CDC), 38, 42, 79, 82, 92–95, 102
chemotherapy, 67, 70, 72
children, with tuberculosis, 38–39, 51, 82–83
cholera, 23

Chopin, Emilia, 21
Chopin, Frédéric, 9–10, 14–15, 16, 17
cilia, 48
Coker, Richard, 87
consumption, 16–18
creosote, 24

detention programs, 20, 75–77, 86–87
diabetes, 34
Directly Observed Therapy, Short Course (DOTS), 73–75, 76, 92, 97
DNA fingerprinting (typing), 106–107
drug-resistant tuberculosis, 26, 28, 36, 45, 54–57, 69–70, 105–106
Dubos, Jean, 18–19
Dubos, René, 18–19, 24, 88

Egypt, ancient, 15
elderly, 33–34
Emerson, Ralph Waldo, 17
endotracheal intubation, 40
ethambutol, 26, 67
extapulmonary tuberculosis, 47–48, 52–53, 66

Fauci, Anthony S., 108
financial costs of tuberculosis, 83–85
Fracastoro, Girolamo, 21
From Chaos to Coercion: Detention and the Control of Tuberculosis (Coker), 87
Galen, 20

Gates, Bill, 96
Gates, Melinda, 96
genetic history, 37–38
germ theory of disease, 22
Global Fund to Fight AIDS,
    Tuberculosis, and Malaria,
    95–96, 102
Global Plan to Stop TB, 92
gold salts, 24
granulomas, 48, 105, 108
Greece, ancient, 16
Guerin, Camille, 60

health-care workers, 34, 39–40,
    56
hemoptysis, 51
Hindus, 16
Hippocrates, 20
Hispanics, 37–38
Histoplasma capsulatum fungus,
    53–54
HIV (human immunodeficiency
    virus), 35–36, 53–54
Hodgkin's disease, 34
Homelessness, 10–11, 36, 44–46,
    73, 111

immigrants, 20, 40–41, 95, 97
immune system, 34–36, 48–50
incentive programs, 72–73
Iseman, Michael, 70, 71, 99
isoniazid, 26, 62, 67, 68, 72

Jackson, Richard, 79, 80
juvenile tuberculosis, 38–39, 51,
    82–83

Keats, John, 17
kidney disease, 34
King's Evil, 16
Koch, Robert, 22, 23, 91

laboratory tests, 66–67

latent infection, 49
leprosy, 47
leukemia, 34
Liszt, Franz, 15
lymph nodes, 48, 52, 53

macrophages, 48
malaria, 7
malnutrition, 33, 35
Mantoux skin test, 22, 32, 49,
    58–59, 61, 62–64
Marten, Benjamin, 21
meat, as source of infection, 47
migrant workers, 37
miliary tuberculosis, 52–53, 68
milk, as source of infection, 19,
    20, 47
minorities, 19–20, 37–38, 81
mortality rates, 17, 20, 26, 28,
    53, 70, 74–75, 83, 91
Mozart, Wolfgang Amadeus, 17
multidrug-resistant tuberculosis
    (MDR-TB), 39, 40, 56–57,
    69–70; treatment of, 69–70
Mycobacterium avium, 47
Mycobacterium bovis, 47, 60
Mycobacterium leprae, 47
Mycobacterium tuberculosis, 8,
    22, 46, 47, 48–50, 54–55

National Institutes of Allergy and
    Infectious Diseases (NIAID),
    108
National Jewish Medical and
    Research Center, 60, 70, 71,
    98–99
Native Americans, 16, 19–20, 37
Neolithic Age, 15
nodules, 50
Noland, Charles, 104
nursing homes, 34

O'Brian, Richard, 109

opium, 21
opportunistic infections, 36
osteopontin, 108–109

patients' rights, 85–87
philanthropy, 95–96
phthisis, 15, 16, 17
Piot, Peter, 83
Pliny the Elder, 21
Pneumocystis carinii fungus, 53
pneumonectomy, 71
Poe, Edgar Allan, 17
polymerase chain reaction (PCR),
    66–67
Portal, Antoine, 17
Pott's disease, 52
primary infection, 48–49
protease inhibitor therapy, 72
pulmonary resection, 71
pulmonary tuberculosis, symp-
    toms of, 50–51
purified protein derivative (PPD),
    62
pyrazinamide, 67, 68, 72

Reichman, Lee, 98
rifabutin, 67, 72
rifampicin, 26, 62, 67, 68, 72
rifamycin, 72
rifapentine, 108
Rifater, 68, 108
Roentgen, Wilhelm K., 65
Rome, ancient, 16, 21, 24
Rothman, David, 87
Russia, 89–91, 90

Sand, George, 18
sanitoriums, 15, 20, 24–26
scrofula, 16, 17
silicosis, 34, 64
skin tests, 22, 32, 49, 58–59, 61,
    62–64, 71
Small, Peter, 42

Snider, Dixie E., 82
spitting, 19
Streptomyces griseus, 26
streptomycin, 26, 27, 67
surgical therapy, 71

TB. *See* Tuberculosis
T-cells, 48
thoracoplasty, 24
Thoreau, Henry David, 17
Trudeau, Edward Livingston, 24
tubercle, 48–50
tuberculin, 22, 61, 62, 71
tuberculosis: antibiotic therapy,
    61–62, 67, 68; case studies,
    9–12, 14–15, 30–31, 44–46,
    58–60, 78–79, 110–113; chal-
    lenges to society of, 79–87;
    children and, 38–39, 51,
    82–83; contagionist theory,
    21–22; detention programs,
    20, 75–77, 86–87; diagnosis
    of, 62–67; Directly Observed
    Therapy, Short Course
    (DOTS), 73–75, 76, 92, 97;
    discrimination and, 19–20; as
    disease of masses, 18–20; drug
    resistant, 26, 28, 36, 45,
    54–57, 69–70, 105–106; early
    remedies, 20–21, 22–26; eld-
    erly and, 33–34; epidemics of,
    17, 37–38; financial costs of,
    83–85; global risk, 41–42;
    government involvement and,
    57, 89–91; health-care work-
    ers and, 39–40; history of,
    15–22, 24–28; HIV and AIDS
    and, 35–36, 53–54, 64, 66,
    71–72, 83; the homeless and,
    10–11, 36, 44–46, 73, 111;
    immigrants and, 20, 40–41,
    95, 97; incentive programs,
    72–73; infection stage, 7,

48–49; isolation for, 20; minorities and, 19–20, 37–38, 81; mortality rates, 17, 20, 26, 28, 53, 74–75, 83, 91; names for, 16; outlook for future, 104–110; poverty and, 36–37, 88; prestige of, 17–18; prisons and, 40, 54, 90, 100–101; resurgence of, 8, 27–29, 80–85; sanitoriums, 15, 20, 24–26; skin testing for, 22, 32, 49, 58–59; stages of, 48–50; surgical therapy, 71; symptoms of, 9, 50–53; transmission of, 32–33, 47; vaccines for, 24, 60–61; X-rays for, 8, 59, 64–66, 100
tuberculous arthritis, 52, 68
tuberculous meningitis, 52, 68

U.S. Agency for International Development (USAID), 95

vaccines, 24, 60–61, 109–110
Valway, Sarah, 82
Villemin, Jean-Antoine, 22
vitamin D, 108

Waksman, Selman, 26, 27
wasting disease, 16
White Plague, 16, 19
White Plague, The (Dubos and Dubos), 18–19
"work cure," 20
World Bank, 75
World Health Organization (WHO), 60, 73, 80, 91–92
World TB Day, 91

X-rays, 8, 59, 64–66

Yamada, Tachi, 103

ABOUT THE AUTHOR

Diane Yancey is the author of more than thirty-five books for middle-grade and high school readers. She has written on topics that range from the Civil War to serial killers. She and her husband live in the Pacfic Northwest with their dog, Gelato, and their three cats, Newton, Lily, and Alice.

PHOTO ACKNOWLEDGMENTS

The images in this book are used with the permission of: © Photopix/Photonica/Getty Images, pp. 3, 7, 14, 30, 44, 58, 78, 88, 104; © SIU/Visuals Unlimited, p. 8; Library of Congress, p. 16 (LC-USZ62-103898); Courtesy of the National Library of Medicine, pp. 23, 27, 35, 65; American Lung Association, pp. 25, 81; © Dieter Telemans/Panos Pictures, p. 39; © David Greedy/Getty Images, p. 43; Centers for Disease Control and Prevention Public Health Image Library/Dr. George P. Kubica, p. 46; © Eric Feferberg/AFP/Getty Images, p. 63; AP Photo/Themba Hadebe, p. 74; © Alex Wong/Getty Images, p. 76; AP Photo/Greg Baker, p. 84; © Jon Spaull/Panos Pictures, p. 90; Centers for Disease Control and Prevention Public Health Image Library/James Gathany, p. 93; AP Photo/Charleston Daily Mail, Craig Cunningham, p. 94; AP Photo/Sharon Farmer, Bill & Melinda Gates Foundation, p. 96; AP Photo/Ed Andrieski, p. 99; © Scientifica/Visuals Unlimited, p. 106, AP Photo/Marcio Jose Sanchez, p. 109.

Front Cover: © S. Lowry/Univ Ulster/Stone/Getty Images (left); © Photopix/Photonica/Getty Images (right).